Jan. 6-2012

To: Ashlee Disston,

Mike Jacobs

Remember,, Never Again "

with all good wishes

Mike Jacobs

Holocaust
Survivor

Have Hope

Believe

and think Positive

ID360370

Holocaust Survivor

MIKE JACOBS' TRIUMPH OVER TRAGEDY

A Memoir

MIKE JACOBS
EDITED BY GINGER JACOBS

EAKIN PRESS ⬧ Austin, Texas

Library of Congress Cataloging-in-Publication Data

Jacobs, Mike, 1925–
    Holocaust survivior : Mike Jacobs' triumph over tragedy / Mike Jacobs ; edited by Ginger Jacobs.— 1st ed.
        p.   cm.
    ISBN 1-56168-543-X
    ISBN 1-57168-472-7 (pbk.)
    1. Jacobs, Mike, 1925– 2. Jews—Poland—Konin (Konin)—Biography. 3. Holocaust, Jewish (1939–1945)—Poland—Konin (Konin)—Personal narratives. 4. Holocaust survivors—Texas—Dallas—Biography. 5. Konin (Konin, Poland)—Biography. 6. Dallas Holocaust Memorial Center. I. Jacobs, Ginger, 1930– II. Title

DS135.P63 J325 2001
943.8'—dc21
[B]
                                    2001023289

FIRST EDITION
Thirteenth Printing
Copyright © 2001
By Mike Jacobs and Ginger Jacobs
Published in the U.S.A.
By Eakin Press
A Division of Sunbelt Media, Inc.
P.O. Drawer 90159 ✒ Austin, Texas 78709-0159
email: eakinpub@sig.net
💻 website: www.eakinpress.com 💻

ISBN 1-57168-543-X HB
ISBN 1-57168-472-7 PB

DEDICATION

I dedicate my book in memory of my family, Jakubowicz:
Father—Mojzesz (Moses)
Mother—Dora
Brother—Avram
Sister—Ryfka
Sister—Ester
Brother—Szlama
who were murdered in the death camp, Treblinka.
To my brother Reuven, who was in the underground and
was killed as a freedom fighter.
And in honor of my present loving family, Jacobs:
Wife—Ginger
Son—Mark
Daughter—Deborah "Debbie" Linksman and
Son-in-law Wayne Linksman
Son—Andrew "Andy"
Son—Reuben.
And to my family, Linksman:
Granddaughter—Rivka
Granddaughter—Leeza
Granddaughter—Sarah
Granddaughter—Aviva.

Our granddaughter, Sarah, wrote this poem while visiting the death camp Treblinka as a participant in the March of the Living program. Mike had asked Sarah to find the Ostrowiec stone as Ostrowiec was the ghetto city he and his family were in before most of his family was sent to Treblinka, where they all perished. At Treblinka, participants were given twenty minutes to write their thoughts. Mike comments, "When I go to Poland, I visit this stone and have a beautiful conversation with my family."

May 1, 2003, 4:10 p.m.

Treblinka Ostrowiec

Dear family I have never met,
This is a time I won't forget.
I know you, but you don't know me,
Let me introduce myself and you will see.
Mendel Jakubowicz is no longer his name,
He had to change it, please don't be ashamed.
There are a few things I would like you to know,
Your son survived and came to America to show.
Great grandma, great grandpa, Michael Jacobs is your son,
He stayed alive to prove the Jews had won.
He visits you often, updates you on his life,
America is great, that is where he met his wife.
Poland is still very deep in his heart,
It's a time in his history he will never part.
He has touched so many lives, inspired them too,
He shares with the world what one human can do.
He is one of the most amazing men on this earth,
He savors everything, and everything its worth.
I am Sarah, the third generation,
Mike never gave up on God's creation.
He married, he has kids, I am his grand-daughter,
I wipe my tears as my eyes water.
I just want you to know Mendel always believed,
Thanks to him my family was received.
You are always with us and we shed our tears,
You will never be forgotten in the years.
A part of you is now with me,
I am taking you to finally witness the land of the free.
                                   —Sarah Linksman

CONTENTS

vi

FOREWORD

It was with a sense of anticipation that I first read these memoirs. I met Mike Jacobs years ago because of his work with survivors and his important efforts to build the Holocaust Museum in Dallas. If you go to the Dallas museum, you meet Mike Jacobs. He is there so often that one is tempted to say always, and his spirit permeates the place. I stood in the railroad car he brought to the United States and understood its power, felt the presence of those who were absent. In the absence, the visitor fills in the smells and the sounds, the heat and the cold, and the trepidation that the Jewish deportees felt on their way to Auschwitz. We later turned to Mike for advice as we contemplated bringing such a boxcar to the United States Holocaust Memorial Museum. He was, as always, enthusiastic and helpful.

I had not known Mike's story, though. I had not even known his Jewish name, Mendel Jakubowicz. I *had* seen his number. I knew that he had entered the "kingdom of night," to use Elie Wiesel's words, and emerged. But in my experience, Mike was not a man of words, but of deeds, less a writer than a talker. He belongs to a breed of men and women who can be found around each of the Holocaust institutions that have been created in the United States. Survivors, teachers, witnesses, they tell their stories, touching the souls, shaping the minds, and kindling the imaginations of the young people they encounter.

It is said that the last words of the renowned Jewish historian Simon Dubnow were, "Write and record." Survivors relate that they made two commitments to those they left behind: to remember, and to not let the world forget. Mike Jacobs has told his story to thousands of people in the past, and now he has recorded his memoir with the help of his American-born wife, Ginger. And for this we must be grateful.

In recent years, three forms of survivor's memoirs have prevailed: the spoken word, the recorded word, and the written word, each with its own strengths and weaknesses. In classrooms throughout the United States and Canada, in museums and educational institutions, survivors are telling their stories to students. The encounter is often electric, and the students regard the survivors as the embodiment of history. They treat them as heroes, which often contrasts markedly with the survivor's own self-image. Powerful as it may be, the lecture is soon over. It passes, and thus its value for historical purposes also wanes. It will have the force of an oral tradition, a tale transmitted and transformed from speaker to listener.

The Fortunoff Archive for Holocaust Testimonies, the Survivors of the Shoah Visual History Foundation, and other oral history projects, have developed a new genre of recorded memory, the videotaped interview. It is a new genre because the technology for it has only existed for the past twenty years. Under Steven Spielberg's leadership, the Shoah Foundation has recorded almost 51,000 interviews in 32 languages in 57 countries, compiling a video documentary record of unprecedented depth and diversity. However, by its nature, the videotaped interview is a one-shot deal; the camera rolls, the survivor speaks, the recording is made. It is too early to tell the impact of this mode of recording Holocaust memoirs, but for the visual, highly technological generation, the potential of these testimonies is quite significant.

Mike has utilized both of these forms of memoir. He has told his story to students and others. He has recorded his testimony. And now he has written a book in which his memories are presented in a detailed narrative, edited and reedited, examined and reexamined.

Jews are a people of the book. Even in the age of the Internet, we still believe in books. Thousands of Holocaust memoirs have been written by survivors, perhaps by now even ten thousand or more. The permanence of written memoirs ensures that the experience they lived is recorded, transmitted and available for generations on end. I respect this work. I revere the moral commitment that underscores this profound commitment to memory.

The permanent written record gives us an opportunity to reflect on the deeper meanings behind survival of the Holocaust. "I had to dream in order to survive," Mike Jacobs tells us. I'm not sure that most readers will grasp how important this statement is, for it truly was Mike's way of coping with the atrocities that he experienced. "I dreamed that I would be free," he says again and again, as a mantra of protest even in Auschwitz.

Gerda Weissman Klein said in the Academy Award–winning film *One Survivor Remembers* that "only those with imagination could survive." She described how for an entire day on a death march she debated whether to wear a red velvet or a blue velvet dress to a party. She preferred blue, but she looked better in red.

Psychologists call this *disassociation*, creating a reality at variance with the one that is being lived. Robert Jay Lifton, the eminent psychiatrist who wrote on the Nazi doctors, termed it *doubling*, the creation of a second self distant from the camp, protected from the environment. Mike did it; so did Gerda. Mike used his dreams and Gerda her imagination to escape, at least for a moment, from the oppressive environment in which they lived.

Mike Jacobs says that "the Nazis could starve and torture my body, but they could never kill my spirit. No matter what they did to me." This, too, is a motif that we find in many survivors' testimonies, and it is a determination that we must respect without daring to judge those who could not endure the torture. Jean Amery has written powerfully of the impact of torture on the victim, and none of us can quite know how we would have endured the ordeal. Primo Levi told of shaving with glass and attempting to stay clean even when he knew it was impossible. Pelagia Lewinska, a Polish non-Jewish survivor, wrote: "They wished to abase us, to destroy our human dignity, to efface every vestige of our humanity . . . to fill us with horror and contempt toward ourselves and our fellows. From the instant when I grasped the motivating principle . . . it was as if I had awakened from a dream. I felt under order to live. And if I did die in Auschwitz, it would be as a human being. I would hold onto my dignity."

What are we to make of Mike's "camp romance" with the girl on the other side of the barbed wire? Viktor Frankl, a prominent psychiatrist who wrote movingly of his own experience in Auschwitz, wrote that the chances of a person surviving the concentration camp psychically intact increased significantly if they could find a sense of meaning—even pretend meaning. Mike Jacobs found his meaning in the romance with a young woman his age with whom he spoke separated by barbed wire. I have no doubt that it contributed to his survival. It gave his life meaning for a time. He made a difference in someone's life. Someone mattered to him.

Creating a sense of meaning and drawing on one's inner strength were essential for survival. Yet there were other factors beyond the victims' control, factors that undoubtedly augment the survivors' gratitude and sense of responsibiity to keep the memory of the Holocaust alive for future generations. We must remember as we read his testimony carefully that Mike had many advantages. He was young. As a rule, only the young and the able-bodied survived. Mike Jacobs could pass as a non-Jew. He spoke Polish fluently. His coloration was light, and thus he could become for a time Marjan Jakubowski. He was therefore able to escape the ghetto and was not deported with most of his family to Treblinka, where 700,000–870,000 were murdered and fewer than 100 Jews survived.

Beyond what this memoir can teach us about individual survival, we also learn something about community. Sociologist Helen Fein writes of the Holocaust that a sacred universe of common obligation was the glue that bound people together. Those inside that common universe felt obligations for one another, not for those on the outside or those who were forced to the margins. Mike Jacobs' experience verifies Fein's observations. Throughout his Holocaust experience, he consistently helped other victims whenever he could.

In the camps, cigarettes and bread were the currency. With

them, almost everything could be bought, and among the most important things that could be bought were shoes. He got shoes for the young woman he saw beyond the barbed wire, and those shoes enabled her to survive. Those unfamiliar with Holocaust literature might wonder what is so important about shoes. Primo Levi wrote: "Death begins with the shoes; for most of us, they show themselves to be instruments of torture, which after a few hours of marching cause painfully sores which become fatally infected. Whoever has them is forced to walk as if he was dragging a convict's chain . . . he arrives late everywhere and everywhere he receives blows. He cannot escape if they run after him. his feet swell and the more the friction with the wood and the cloth of the shoes becomes insupportable."

Of the death marches, Gerda Klein said: "I saw some girls breaking off their toes like twigs." So something as simple as a good pair of shoes was a secret of survival. The basic gesture of Mike giving his "pretend" girlfriend a pair of shoes made all the difference in the world.

As a recorder of history, Mike gives us some important evidence about the killers. He does not paint the Germans with a single brush. He could differentiate between Sergeant Holzer, a cruel sadist who cared for his wife and children and yet could kill other men's wives and other parents' children, seemingly without conflict, and a German soldier who served his country but hated Hitler, with whom Mike could trade for arms. Daniel Jonah Goldhagen has written an important book depicting the killers and their willing participation in the Nazi program of "exterminationist anti-Semitism." Yet Mike Jacobs and other survivors report that they could distinguish between the Germans. In fact, an uncanny ability to size up people was essential to Mike's survival during the war, especially in the camps, and to his success in the United States, where he made his living in the salvage business.

Mike also gives important information about the bystanders. Here, too, he knew whom to trust and when. He understood that one could not overstay one's welcome, and that even within a family, a husband could be anti-Semitic while his wife was gracious.

We learn a bit about resistance from this memoir. Mike

Jacobs does not glamorize his role, but if he could not openly resist, he defied the Nazis and even sabotaged production when given the opportunity to do so.

Mike Jacobs has given meaning to his survival by his deeds, by what he has created in Dallas. He has given purpose to his survival by creating a loving family, children, and now grand-children. He has borne witness through the spoken word, and now in the written word. It is our task to accept his testimony with gratitude and become the witnesses of the witnesses.

MICHAEL BERENBAUM
DIRECTOR, U.S. HOLOCAUST
RESEARCH INSTITUTE
LOS ANGELES, CALIFORNIA

EDITOR'S NOTE

In writing this book, Mike has related his memoirs of his Holocaust experience through the use of transcribed tapes of his story as told to many audiences, in interviews, and by dictation. He speaks as a teenager because he was a teenager during the war years. His English is somewhat different from that spoken by people born in the United States. (When he speaks to groups, he always quips about his Texas accent.) In editing Mike's story, I have tried to retain the integrity of his speech patterns and vocabulary, as well as expressions.

I think that his ability for total recall of what he has endured, along with his willingness to relate it, is rather remarkable. Not only has he always been consistent in his recounting of his personal history, other sources have reaffirmed his accurate recall. As he was the youngest child of a loving family, I think he must have had an extremely secure childhood. The apparently close relationships of his extended family and warm childhood memories have certainly had a part in forming his positive attitude toward life.

His mission continues as he speaks to multitudes of students, organizations, churches, synagogues, institutions, and professional, service, civic, and business groups—to anyone who will listen. Over the years, he has spoken to about 500,000 people. He has aided therapists in working with groups, as well as individuals with eating disorders, drug problems, and emotional problems. He has also changed the attitudes of some skin-heads and other neonazis who have heard him speak. Some of them have written striking letters thanking Mike for his insights and their impact, which helped them to change their behavior. (See Appendix 3, page 195). Mike's triumph over tragedy continues to have its effect and serves as an inspiration to all who hear him.

GINGER JACOBS
JANUARY 2001

SPECIAL NOTE TO STUDENTS

A special thanks to the many students who have asked Mike to write this book about his Holocaust experience and survival. Mike's story is the history of the Holocaust as he experienced it, some of which historians have drawn on. In writing history books, they have referred to incidents that Mike lived and included in this memoir. I have therefore included two of their books in which he was quoted, and others, in the notes and bibliography. It is your challenge to remember and act on what you have learned from Mike and the lessons of history.

GINGER JACOBS, EDITOR
JANUARY 2001

ACKNOWLEDGMENTS

Special thanks to Jamie Specht, who first heard me speak when she was a junior high school student. Several years later, Jamie, as a junior in 1980 at Berkner High School, came to interview me. After I received the Hope for Humanity Award in 1994 from the Dallas Memorial Center for Holocaust Studies, Jamie urged me to write my story and followed me to many of my presentations with tape recorder in hand. My sons, Mark and Andy, had also taped their interviews of me when they were high school students, as well as Ginger, my wife, who taped many of my presentations. Jamie then transcribed the tapes from which this book has emerged. I am forever grateful to Jamie.

Thanks to Michael Berenbaum, our good friend and supporter, who also encouraged me to write my memoir, read the manuscript, and graciously accepted my request to write the foreword.

Thanks to Debbie Winegarten, who worked in a professional capacity with the manuscript and named many of the chapters of the book.

A special thanks to our cousin, Melanie Spiegel, of Photocom Inc. for making the services of photographer Phillip Esparza, and his assistant, Jay Conlon, available to us for the cover photo. Melanie was very gracious, as were Phillip and Jay, which we deeply appreciate. Phillip is a gifted photographer with whom we enjoyed working.

Thanks to Dr. Ron Marcello, director of the University of

North Texas Oral History Program, and to Keith Rosen, a student of Dr. Marcello, who interviewed me in 1989.

Our thanks to dear friends and family who have encouraged us, proofread, made suggestions, helped with computer glitches, and some "hand holding," including:

Theo Richmond, a good friend whom we first met when he was writing his book *Konin, A Quest.*

Ruthe Winegarten, who read an early version of the manuscript and has continually encouraged us with this project.

Jackie Waldman, who initially put the sequence of events of my oral-history interview in order.

Phyllis and Herbert Kadish, for their hospitality and "being there for us."

Granddaughters Rivka, Leeza, Sarah, and Aviva—with special thanks to Leeza, who greatly helped with her computer skills.

Children Mark, Debbie, Andy, and Reuben.

Computer gurus: Son-in-law Wayne Linksman and friends, Carolyn Zalta, Gordon and Cookie Peadon.

Ruth Brodsky, Gladys Leff, and Harriet Gross.

The many teachers and students who have asked and encouraged me to write my book.

A special and warm thanks to Joe Funk of Joe Funk Construction Company for his professionalism and friendship in building the Dallas Memorial Center for Holocaust Studies. He was a pleasure to work with.

A special thanks to architects Cole Smith and Robert Ekblad of the architectural firm Smith Ekblad & Associates for their excellent job in designing The Dallas Memorial Center for Holocaust Studies, now called The Dallas Holocaust Memorial Center. We appreciate their consideration, sensitivity, and artistry. It was a pleasure to work with them.

Our thanks and appreciation to the late Ed Eakin, and to publisher Virginia Messer, editor Angela Buckley, and the staff at Eakin Press. They have been receptive, sensitive, and gracious in working with us on this book.

With heartfelt appreciation to all of you,
MICHAEL "MIKE" JACOBS and GINGER JACOBS
JANUARY 2001

PART I

Growing Up in Konin

– 1 –

I Had Lots of
Relatives

KONIN, POLAND, 1925–1939. Today everybody calls me Mike Jacobs, but I was born Mendel Jakubowicz in a small Polish town, Konin, about 120 miles from Warsaw, not too far from the German border. Konin was a very old town of about 12,000 people, with about 3,500 Jews. The town was mostly Catholic, in keeping with the general Polish Catholic population. The rest of the population was Protestant and Jewish. It was a very pretty town. We had a large, beautiful park with a small lagoon with a narrow bridge over the lake. We could stand on the bridge and see the various fish as they swam in the lake. We enjoyed feeding the fish. There were deer in a fenced area of the park. The park also had a gazebo in it. The town orchestra played concerts in the park as well. The city hall was a distinctive building with its tall clock tower. The town emblem was a horse. Jews settled there in 1397.

We had a wonderful Jewish community. We had a very old and beautiful *shul* [synagogue, house of worship]. Most of the Jews lived in the surrounding neighborhood so they could walk to the shul on *Shabbos* [Sabbath, Saturdays] and *Yom Tov* [Jewish holidays]. We had a Jewish committee called the *Geminde*, which took care of many things. The Geminde paid our cantor, the rabbi, and for the upkeep of the shul. In the old days, we had poor transient Jewish beggars going door to door to door. But the Geminde finally decided to open a shelter for them so they would have clean beds and a place to sleep. Then the next morning they gave them some *zlotys* [money] and told them to go on their way.

We also had a *shtibel,* a small house of learning where the *Hasidim,* the really Orthodox Jews, prayed. There were additional small *shtibelach* [plural of shtibel] with groups of ten or twenty families who worshiped there.

My family was religious, liberal Orthodox, and we kept *kosher* [in accordance with Jewish dietary laws]. Some Jews were more liberal Orthodox than others. At home, we were more liberal. We did not wear the side curls worn by Hasidic Jews, and nobody wore beards. My father would go to shul every morning and evening for the religious services, and always on Saturday mornings and Jewish holidays.

My grandmother on my mother's side died before I was born. I remember my grandfather on my mother's side, Herman Stein, only very vaguely. I never knew my grandparents on my father's side. My grandfather Stein was already very old when I was born. He was retired then, living on the income from a rent house. He was not a rich man, but he was a very religious person. He had a shtibel in his home where people used to come on Friday nights and Saturday and pray. He came to our house on Friday nights for Sabbath dinner. Before he retired, my grandfather had a freight business with horses and wagons. Before World War I, part of Poland was occupied by Russia and part by Germany; Konin was on the Russian side. My grandfather delivered merchandise to the German side and then brought back materials to our city. Once, when my grandfather had a helper driving the horses, my oldest brother, who was nine at the time, jumped on the wagon but fell off when the wagon went over a bump or a pothole in the road. A wagon wheel ran over him, and my brother was killed. My parents never discussed him at home, but I found out about him from a neighbor, since he died before I was born. He was buried near the front of the cemetery just inside the gate. Although I had seen his name on the tombstone, it had never dawned on me that he was my brother.

My mother, Dora, had three sisters, all living in Konin. Her sisters were Rosa, Ester, and Haya. My mother was not the oldest, but was the peacemaker in the family. My mother also had a brother, Reuven, who lived in London but died at a young age, leaving a widow and five sons.

Ciotka [aunt] Chaya was married to Shmuel Hollander, and they had sons Aaron and Yitzchak, and a daughter, Rosa, who married Zalman Richke. They were tailors.

Ciotka Ester was married to Szlomo Szwam [pronounced "shwam"], who made horse harnesses. He made beautiful harnesses. Their children were Avram Meir, Lotka, Moshe, and Shana. Ciotka Rosa had been widowed for many years. Her four children were Avram, Shlomo, Pearl, and Rachel.

Although my mother was traditional Jewish, she was liberal in her thinking.

She wore a *sheytl* [a wig], as was the custom for married women. She had two shetyls, one for the weekdays, and a *shabbesdikeh* one [for Saturdays and holidays]. I remember she kept the wig on a wooden block, and when it needed curling and waving, I took it to the woman who looked after the shetyls. One of my jobs was to take the holiday wig on Friday. The woman had lots of wigs on wooden blocks. I carried my mother's shetyl to and from her shop in a cardboard box.

I went to my Aunt Rosa's grocery store often, because we used to buy lots of flour, herring, sugar, and other things from her and her daughter Pearl. On Saturday afternoons, Aunt Rosa used to give me an apple. This was a big thing. Aunt Rosa was a very religious woman. Her hands were always cracked from digging the herring packed in brine out of the barrels. Because Aunt Rosa was very religious, she wore a wig, in keeping with Jewish tradition for married women. She was so religious that she read the Bible on Saturday afternoons. She was a fairly well-to-do widow, who bought her older son, Szlomo, a Chevrolet car to be used as a taxi. She figured he could make a better living as a taxi driver. He took people to and from the railroad station. As his prices were so low, he could not make a living. He parked the car in my grandfather's courtyard, and I would get into the car and pretend I was driving. I played there very often and can still see the car in my mind's eye. Later, Szlomo leased a fruit orchard and sold the fruit.

Another of Aunt Rosa's sons, Avram, was a tailor. Avram was the only one of his family to survive the war.

My father had a brother, Uria, and two sisters, Chaya Sara and Rosa, that I knew. My father's sister Chaya Sara, whom we called Ha'sara, was married to Uncle Mordicai. She had a general store where she sold dry goods [cloth], as well as groceries. She and Uncle Mordicai also had a big farm. They raised wheat, potatoes, and oats. They had nine children, two sons and seven daughters. When I was on school vacation, during the day I would go with my cousin Szlomo to their farm outside Tuliszkow, a small town about thirteen kilometers [seven miles] from Konin. We would hitch the horse to the wagon and load the plow in the wagon. Uncle Mordicai's horse was twenty years old and very mean. He used to kick. My cousin Szlomo would plow, and I used to follow and watch him plow. After the harvest, Szlomo and I used to stay in the field at night and watch that no one would steal the wheat. All the cousins would go and harvest the wheat, and we brought it into the barn. Later, we thrashed the wheat by hand. We had a stick attached with a leather strap to another long piece of wood. We would hit the wheat so that the kernels would fall out. Next we gathered the kernels together and sifted them. We cousins then took the grains to the flour mill and sold them to the mill. I had a good time.

My father's brother Uria was very unlucky, but he had a beautiful daughter. Sometimes he came to see my father, and my father would give him some money. My father was quiet, and a good man. He would give everything away when he had it. My father shared what he had with his brother in Tuliszkow. Another of father's brothers, who was well-off, lived in a nearby town, Kleczew, about twenty-five kilometers [fifteen miles] from Konin, but that uncle died at an early age, leaving sons and daughters. His son Yecheil was the oldest. We had lots of cousins, but I didn't know all of them.

Some of my cousins on my father's side lived in Lask. Lask was about one hundred kilometers [sixty miles] from Konin. Who could travel that far? It was far away from us, and so I did not get to meet them. My cousin Tova Jakubowicz [pronounced "ya-ka-bow-vitch"] Dan survived the war, and I met her in Germany after the war. Of my uncle Mordicai and aunt Chaya Sara's children, Henek Gerson left Poland before I was born. Another, Ester Gerson, left for South Africa in the 1930s, and before she left we had a big feast. Everybody was happy for her. Another cousin, Szlomo Gerson, survived the concentration camps and joined his siblings in South Africa. When his older sister, Regina, got married in Tuliszkow, we were invited to the wedding. We could not afford to go, so they sent a taxi for my parents. It was very special. I wanted to go to the wedding, so I hid between their legs on the floor of the back seat. After the wedding, I wanted to stay with Aunt Rosa in Tuliszkow. I ate at Aunt Ha'sara's house in Tuliszkow because I liked her food better. Of the children who remained in Europe, only Szlomo survived the war.

We had a big family with lots of relatives, and most of them lived in Konin, so we saw them a lot. My aunts and uncles were very close to my family. My mother's three sisters were close to me, as well as the rest of the family. Aunt Rosa and her husband, Avraham Markowski, lived in Tuliszkow, with their two sons, Yacheil and Yaakov, and their daughter, Kalcza. The boys were tailors, too. Since Tuliszkow was in farm country, they sold to the farmers. The farmers sometimes paid for their clothes with chickens and geese. My uncle, Uria Jakubowicz, lived in Tuliszkow and was a tanner, a very poor man. Another of my father's brothers, Uncle Meyer, lived in Kleczew. He was a widower and had six children, Yecheil, Szlomo, Yoseph, Adela, Yetka, and Sala. The sons made beautiful sheepskin coats. They would go to surrounding towns and sell at the open markets. Sometimes they came to Konin to sell their goods.

My oldest brother, Avram, born in 1909, was a very quiet person and very devoted to the family. He had dark hair, heavy eyebrows, and was of average height. My brother Szlama, born in 1916, was very sports-minded, always active in sports such as soccer, broad jump, high jump, the 100- and 400-meter dash, and gymnastics. He was tall and had brown hair. My brother Reuven, born in 1919, was six years older than I. He was tall, blond, and more intellectual. He read books all the time and had many discussions about the books with his circle of friends. He was in the Zionist organization. There were always two or three boys sitting around reading books with him, and then they would review them.

My sisters were like any other girls. Ester, born in 1914, was engaged to Wolf Kaczka, a tailor, before the war. Wolf made custom clothes for women. They had already bought furniture for their apartment, which was beautiful, much nicer than our furniture was. I remember it like it was today. They had a big living room, which they would have used for a workshop during the day, and a nice kitchen. They were later married in the Ostrowiec [pronounced os-tro-vitz] ghetto, but never got to move into their apartment in Konin.

My oldest sister, Ryfka, born in 1911, was a seamstress who made shirts for the stores. She bought clothes for herself with the money she earned. She was very well dressed, tall, and had beautiful legs. One of the department stores wanted her to sit in the store window and model their silk stockings, but my mother told her "No," and no it was, although Ryfka could have made lots of money doing it.

Everybody got a Jewish education. I started going to *cheder*, religious school, where I also learned to read Hebrew, when I was four years old. When I was six, my brothers decided that I should be in the choir. They had to chase me around a few blocks to catch me, because I didn't want to go. I had to go to the shul to let the cantor hear what kind of voice I had. I had a very strong soprano, and the cantor told me that I would sing in the choir, where I sang for six years. My brothers Reuven and Szlama also sang in the choir; Szlama was a baritone, and Reuven was a soprano, but when he was older he went over to alto.

My whole family was musical. My father played a very good violin, viola, and trumpet. A picture of him and a friend, both in Russian uniforms, hung on the wall over the bed; they had both played in the Tzar's orchestra in Moscow when they were in the Russian military. My father was drafted into the Russian army and had to stay there for six years (this was when Poland was part of Russia). He was a very good violinist, until one day the small finger of his left hand would not straighten out. He still played the violin and the trumpet.

My father wanted me to learn to play the violin, so every morning he would stand in front of my bed and tap his foot in a waltz beat, 1-2-3, 1-2-3. I would practice by myself upstairs where my cousins lived, as it was quieter there. I was planning to take free violin lessons at school, but the school was not able to get a violin teacher, so the lessons were not given, but I continued to practice at home.

One summer day when I was practicing, I looked out the window and saw some street musicians playing. I ran down the stairs to hear the street musicians play. As I was jumping down the stairs, I caught the back of my heel on one of the steel cross rods that were placed along the corner beneath and across the stair. My heel began bleeding, and I was screaming. My family took me to Dr. Bulka, who sewed my heel up. He said I was very lucky, because if I had cut it one-tenth of a millimeter deeper, I would have cut the main artery and would have lost my foot. I spent the rest of my summer vacation in bed and on crutches.

When I went back to school that fall, I had to write a paper about how I spent my summer vacation. I wrote about my accident, and the teacher gave me a very bad grade, a two. I could not understand why I got that grade. When I questioned the teacher, she said that I had written a fantasy. I told her it was the truth and asked if she would like to see my scar. I took off my shoe and sock and showed her the big red cut, which still had the stitches in it, and she changed my grade to a five [the highest grade, like getting an A].

In Poland, it was very hard to get a higher education. Before my time, we had a very good Jewish *gymnasium* [like a high school]. I was told that the Polish government closed it because they did not want to accredit it.

Avram became an apprentice to a very good tailor. After about three years of apprenticeship, he took an exam in Lodz to get his master tailor certification. That enabled him to take apprentices and teach them to become tailors. My mother bought a sewing machine, and Avram opened a workshop in our house. My brother Szlama also learned to be a tailor. Avram, Szlama, and two more apprentices made suits and overcoats for the big department stores. The department stores supplied the material. Avram designed the suits and overcoats. He then made the patterns and cut the material for the garments, but sent the pants to our cousin to sew, as it helped him to also make a living. As a master tailor, Avram became the breadwinner for the family. The department stores wanted him to make their garments because he was so good—he had "the touch," and he made his own designs. Avram and Szlama's workshop was prosperous.

For shoes we went to the shoemakers. When I went to Germany after the war, I couldn't understand how people bought shoes in a department store. We always went to the shoemaker, who measured our foot and crafted custom-made shoes.

Reuven was more interested in books and organizational work, but he had to have a profession to support himself. Reuven worked for a man who made the leather tops for shoes. He could also design shoes. He would have been a great shoemaker and a designer had he been in the United States. When anti-Semitism started to grow in Konin, they opened a Polish-owned department store with the most modern shoes. I don't know where the merchandise came from, maybe Germany or Paris or Italy. Reuven would go and copy the shoes in the store windows. When the Polish storekeepers saw my brother coming, they pulled the curtains over the show windows so that he couldn't copy their beautiful designs. Reuven first worked as an apprentice for a person who made the tops for the shoes to sell to shoemakers. The shoemakers then combined them with soles to make the finished shoes for stores. We made a good living until 1939, when the war started. If the war had not broken out, our family would have had our own clothing store with both men's and women's clothes.

Activities and Household

KONIN, POLAND, 1925–1939. Every Friday, my mother went to the department store to collect the money for the finished coats and suits. She brought it all home. She then gave Avram enough money so that he could go out on Saturday night to the movies with friends or take a girlfriend out. If Avram had money left from the weekend, he gave it back to mother. Szlama also got his money from mother. Reuven and I went to the Zionist organization, where we used to sing, dance, and play Ping-Pong.

When I was a kid and came home from school with nothing to do, my brothers would let me do some sewing. I sewed the lining by hand into the sleeves of coats. I knew I was going to be a tailor, but I didn't want to work for the department stores. I wanted to be on my own. I decided that I would buy the material, take the pants we would make, and go out and sell them at the market. The farmers also brought their goods to the market twice a week, on Tuesdays and Fridays. They especially came on Fridays, because all the Jewish people would buy eggs in the morning to make *challah* [twisted egg bread made for Sabbath], cake, and other baked goods, and they would buy chickens, geese, or ducks for Sabbath dinner. I told my family that when I finished grammar school we were going to have our own store, and I would go to high school at night.

My sister Ryfka got pre-cut material from the little department store, from which she sewed shirts. She was paid by the piece. My sister Ester helped take care of our home. Ester helped our mother with the household duties—scrubbing the floors, washing the clothes, darning the socks. On wash day, we had to heat the water on the stove, fill up the wash basin, scrub the clothes on the washboard, and hang the clothes in our attic or outside in the small courtyard. Then, when they were dry, we took them over to the person who had a mangle machine, which passed them through heated rollers to be ironed. We always had warm, clean clothes.

When my parents first married, my father was a tanner. He bought the hides of cows or young horses, pickled them with brine or vinegar, cleaned them up, and then sold the skins to make leather for shoe tops. He later gave up this business, as it wasn't profitable. He tried to bring in merchandise from another tanner, in the city of Kolo. At first he bought a horse and wagon, which he drove himself. He later leased the horse and wagon and had a farmer drive them. He didn't have to work so hard then and had fewer worries. His business was being a spiriture, like "pick up and delivery." During the summers, I sometimes went with him on trips to neighboring towns. On the way home, we often stopped at a little forest, and I picked blackberries. Oh, they were so delicious!

I also remember going with my father to Kalisz, a town about fifty-two kilometers [about thirty miles] from Konin, to deliver live fish, carp. We had to stop en route at the pump in the square of Rychwal, a town about eighteen kilometers [about twelve miles] from Konin, and put fresh water in the barrels to keep them alive before delivering the fish on Friday morning so they could be prepared before Sabbath. He got twenty-five zloty for hauling the fish. He also bought rabbits and ermines and took them to the person who skinned them. Only the rich people could afford ermine. My father delivered these types of goods to some stores in Konin for two or three years before the war; then he retired when he was in his early sixties. By this time, my brothers were making enough money so he didn't have to work. They wanted him to rest, but he wouldn't. Sometimes he would rent a horse and wagon from a farmer, drove to Kolo with orders from the stores in Konin to pick up goods, and bring them back to Konin to deliver to the stores. He had letters with him authorizing him to pick up merchandise and deliver it back to the stores in Konin.

My family was very close, and I think that was because of my mother. She was the disciplinarian, and my father's role was to make money and bring it home to support the family. We children never disagreed with our parents. My mother was a giving and loving person. She could give, but she couldn't take. She was also like a mother to her sisters. When her sisters had a problem, they came to her, and she settled their arguments.

Our house was an apartment with two bedrooms and a kitchen. During the day, one of the bedrooms, with two beds, became the workshop. My two sisters slept together, two of my brothers slept together, Avram slept with my father, and I slept with my mother until I was ten or twelve years old. I later slept on a small couch. Sure, it was crowded, but we did not know anything else. There were five families living in our apartment house. We heated our apartment with coal and wood. The kitchen in our apartment was very small, and sometimes there was a bed in there, too.

Since water was not piped in, we had outhouses and bathed in a round steel tub with hot water once a week, on Fridays before Sabbath. Between times, we washed ourselves with cold water in big basins. We cleaned our teeth using our fingers and salt. I didn't have a toothbrush and toothpaste. Once, when I had a cavity, instead of going to the dentist I took some cotton and iodine and pushed it in to burn the cavity out. It hurt a long time, but then it stopped. We did not get teeth filled with silver—who could afford it? Sometimes, people who could not afford to go to the dentist wrapped their swollen faces with a shawl to keep them warm. We pulled teeth by tying a string on the door, putting it around the tooth, and then, boom, shut the door, and the tooth came out! Sometimes I wiggled my loose tooth around with my finger until it came out.

Outhouses were in the courtyards, and some were cleaner than others. I was always afraid of the rats in the outhouse. They were terrible. My older brother Szlama was good at throwing bricks at them, so he was my protector.

Sometimes I went to the town pump, which was near one of the small town squares and about a block from our house, to bring water home to my family. Pumping the water was easy compared to carrying the buckets of water home. The rich people had water carriers to bring them water. The carriers had a yoke that fit over their shoulders on which to hold the buckets of water. I had to carry a bucket in each hand. We also had a rain barrel to catch the rain for washing my sisters' hair, as the water made their hair soft and shiny.

I was a mischievous kid, and when I got into trouble my mother spanked me. My father never spanked me. Sometimes my brothers disciplined me, too, with a *klop* [hit]. I was the youngest, and I was spoiled. I got away with lots of things. I was always active in sports—gymnastics, track and field. I could never be quiet except at cheder and in public school. There, I did respect the teachers, but outside, I was jumping around—even off the roof. We swam in the Warta [pronounced "varta"] River, which was close by. I had to teach myself how to swim, and once, when I got out in the current, it pulled me under. I don't know how I got back up, but I did. After that, I was a little scared to play around in the water.

When I came home for lunch, I opened the door and asked, "What's for lunch?" If I didn't like what we had, I said, "I want soup." Mother always made soup. I always loved soup and still do.

We did not have a radio at home. When we wanted to listen to the radio, we went down to what used to be the pub, where the owner had a big radio. I think it was a Phillips, and everybody used to listen over there. We stood outside and listened to the news to find out what was going on.

My first language was Yiddish, which we spoke at home. I had to learn Polish because I had to go to school, and when you live in a country, you have to learn to speak their language. I only went to the fifth grade in that public school, which was attended only by Jewish kids, since it was in a Jewish neighborhood. After the fifth grade, the government desegregated the school; five of us boys and five girls were sent to a different public school, which was run by Catholics with mostly Catholic teachers. They "bussed" me—by foot—to the Polish public school. Although boys and girls went to the same school, they were separated in different parts of the building. There were ten of us chosen to go to the school where only Poles went, at the edge of the city. We were in school five or six hours a day, and then we had the summer off, and we took off for the Jewish holidays even when we went to the Polish school.

It was cold in the winter. I went to the secular school from early in the morning until twelve or one in the afternoon. After that, I went home for lunch. Then I went to Hebrew school until six or seven at night. I did my homework at night after I got home, but I did not turn on the lights, because it was expensive. I took out the kerosene lamp.

At the Polish school, sometimes we had fights because the gangs of Polish boys wanted extortion money to protect us. I never gave them anything, because I said it is better that I fight than to give them what I have. My friends used to bring five *groszy* [pennies], and that was a lot of money. I could have gone to the candy store and bought a whole sack full of candies or a big ice cream cone for those five groszy. My parents worked too hard for our things to give them away. I would fight the boys one on one, and once I hit the leader and gave him a black eye. The boy's father was the janitor in my uncle's building. When he found out what his son had done, he spanked him so hard my uncle could hear him from upstairs.

At the public school, in every classroom there was a picture of President Moscicki of Poland on the wall, and in the middle was a crucifix. A picture of Field Marshall Pilsudski was on the other side. Everyone stood up in the morning to say prayers before classes started. We five Jewish boys who were in the class were silent and did not pray. When the priests came for religious classes, we were excused. The other students would complain, "Why are the Jewish students being excused, and we have to sit here for two hours and listen to religious instruction?" The priests told them that we prayed to a different God and that we went to our own religious school. When they had religious studies, we left to go to our school, the Hebrew school. The Catholic boys did not understand. They felt that we should be the same.

They resented us for being different. I believed we should all respect each other.

We had lots of homework. Sometimes I studied very late at night by the kerosene lamp. It was hard on my eyes. Or I would get up very early at three or four o'clock in the morning and open the book and read. Sometimes my brothers and sisters helped me. One of my Jewish friends was one of the best students in the whole school and was a tremendous mathematician. Sometimes I asked him to explain things to me.

I liked history very much. When it was parents' day at school, my teacher said to me, "You know, Mendel, you never study at home."

"Sure I study," I said.

"Oh, no," the teacher said. You listen to the other students, and you catch on right away. I give you lots of credit for how you can twist things around."

3

Holidays

KONIN, POLAND, 1925–1939. There was always anti-Semitism in our city. Where I came from in Poland was the cradle of anti-Semitism. Even though I was only a kid, I could feel that we were second-class citizens. The anti-Semites did not do anything to me, but I remember they used to go around before the war and tell the Polish people not to buy from Jewish stores. All of a sudden, some Poles opened a store supported by anti-Semites, either a very rich person or a group. They said, "Don't buy from the Jews. The Jews are pigs, the Jews are thieves, they are Christ killers."

One day a bunch of non-Jewish guys from neighboring villages were about to come into our town. They were carrying clubs and big sticks. We knew them to be anti-Semitic. We Jewish people knew there was going to be trouble. My brother Szlama and his friends, whom we called the "1916ers," as all of them were born in 1916, were tall, well-built gymnasts. They went to confront the thugs. They approached the anti-Semitic group at the end of the bridge as the group was crossing over the Warta River and told them that if they crossed the bridge they would never get back. The thugs turned around, and everything was quiet. After that incident, we had no more problems.

I played outside with the Polish kids when we went to school with them, although there were many Jews in the neighborhood. We all lived in the same neighborhood. Sometimes the Poles and the Jews lived in the same apartment building, as some of the Poles were janitors.

In Poland, when you finished the seventh grade, it was like finishing high school or more here in the United States. Very few people went that far. If some students made four or five grades they were lucky. Either they failed, or when they reached the age of eleven or twelve their parents took them out of school to go to work, or made them work at home to help support the family. The Jewish people had a hard life; only a few Jewish families were rich. But everyone in my family except Reuven finished the seventh grade. He did not finish because he was sick for two years with some kind of poisoning he got from eating green apples.

Our doctor was Dr. Joel. When Dr. Joel died, an orchestra played, and businesses closed as the funeral procession passed by. He was very respected by everyone in Konin. When he visited a poor sick person, he always left money to buy medicine. When his hearse, which was pulled by horses, approached the shul, the orchestra stopped playing.

My mother was a wonderful cook, the best of all her sisters. My aunts learned everything they knew from her. Everything she made was so tasty and so good, and she was never stingy with the ingredients. My other aunts had money, but they were stingy. My cousins used to ask my mother, "Aunt Dora, why are you making the cake so good? It's always so nice and yellow, with lots of eggs and butter. It is delicious."

When mother served chicken soup, she had to be careful that none of the pieces of vegetables were floating around, or my brother Avram wouldn't eat it. If the soup got overcooked and white, nobody would eat it. There was never any food left over, except maybe the soup.

The only place we had to store food was in the basement, because it was cool down there. We didn't have refrigeration, but we had ice. Mr. Green, who owned the soda factory, hired people in the winter to go to the river to cut out the blocks of ice that had formed. They brought them back to the warehouse and covered them with sawdust. They stayed frozen through the summer. We bought our blocks of ice from Mr. Green to make ice cream in the summer. Those blocks of ice sure were heavy, but I got paid for stacking them. In the winter, our basement was full of potatoes, and my mother used to take cabbage, put it in a wooden barrel, put a top over it and a heavy stone on the top of the cover, and make sauerkraut. We used wood and coal to heat our house in the winter. We would bring a little stove in the kitchen and put a pipe around the room, and all the neighbors used to come to our house and sit in the warm kitchen after supper. Then they would go home to the cold.

When I would go to bed in the winter, I used to go out from the hot little kitchen into an unheated room. I jumped into bed and curled up like a ball. Slowly, little by little, I used to stretch myself out until the bed warmed up. It was COLD. I also remember we used to warm up the dough for the challah in the bed. We put the bowl with the dough in the bed and covered it with a towel so it would be warm enough for the dough to rise. I had to be very careful not to push it out with my feet when I stretched, because it was under the covers getting warm. The bedcovers were made from down, so they were very light and warm. In the morning, my mother would take the dough out, make the challah, and send it to the bakery. When we got up in the mornings, it was so cold we jumped out from bed and dressed fast. Can you imagine? Fifteen degrees below zero outside and not have heat?

Food was precious. We didn't just cut a loaf of bread into lots of pieces. My mother would cut one piece for breakfast, another piece for lunch, and then a third piece for dinner.

Life was beautiful because I had a loving family. Some of my cousins would come over to our house. Their family was much richer than ours was, because their father had brothers in the United States who used to send dollars. Our house was always open for everybody. My mother was a good lady.

The holidays at home were always a big occasion. Everybody dressed up in his or her best clothes. I sat close to my father in shul, or I sat in the back. Everyone used to have his or her own seat.

My mother made the challah herself every Friday for Sabbath. About four weeks before Passover, mother leased a bakery, *kashered* it [cleansed and prepared the store], and had about

twenty people, men and women, make the *matzah*, the special
unleavened bread eaten on Passover. The women would take
a piece of the dough and roll it into large, round, flat pieces.
After the women rolled the dough into pieces, one of the men
would take the flat pieces to a different table. I often helped the
other men use a small tool that had a wheel with sharp points,
which we rolled over the flattened dough to make little rows of
holes in the dough. The pieces were then taken to the oven,
where they quickly baked and had no time to rise. They were
then stacked and taken to the store to be sold to the Jews of the
city and surrounding towns. She also made matzah meal from
the crumbs of the matzah. She would arrange for the poor to
come pick up their matzahs and the matzah meal for free. So as
not to embarrass the poor, mother made special packages for
them to pick up.

Our family celebrated Passover together to the letter. We
didn't finish our *Seder* [the special Passover service during the
meal of the first two nights] until one o'clock in the morning, and
I would ask the four questions: "Why is this night different from
all other nights? Why on this night do we eat only matzah, which
is unleavened bread? Why on this night must we eat bitter herbs?
Why on this night do we dip our herbs twice and recline at the
table?" I used to fall asleep before the service was over.

On Chanukah we had evening services where we lit the
Chanukah candles. I sang in the choir as we sang *Ha-Nerot-Ha-
Lalu* [a special blessing over the candles at the service]. We also
lit the candles at home. On *Simchat Torah* [the holiday of
Rejoicing over the reading of the Five Books of Moses] we got
flags with an apple and a candle on top. We marched around the
shul as the elders carried the scrolls of the Five Books of Moses.
Some of the women threw candy from the balcony as we
marched around.

Friday night, which began our Sabbath, at home was nice.
It made no difference how much you had or how poor, you
always had enough to eat. We had a white tablecloth and beautiful silver candelabras. There was not enough room to sit at the
table, so we pulled a sliding shelf out of the credenza. I used to
sit with my sister at the credenza, and the whole family sang
after our meal. We were a very, very happy family. My father, who

had a good voice, always chanted the *Kiddush* [sanctification prayer over the wine]. For Sabbath we had carp and some other, smaller fish. My mother browned and stuffed the carp. But sometimes we had sweet and sour fish. We always knew if it was Friday or a holiday, because we could smell the fish cooking. After that we had noodles, chicken soup, and later we had meat and spinach and peas. Every week it was the same thing. After eating our meal, we sat around and sang. We had three people who sang in the choir. My mother and my sisters had good voices, and my father had a tremendous voice. The neighbors would stand outside the window listening to us sing. We had a good time singing songs in Yiddish and Hebrew.

On Saturday mornings, my father, my brother Reuven, and I went to shul. The rest of my brothers sometimes went, but they stood in the back to show respect for my father. Since Jews are not supposed to cook on the Sabbath, the more Orthodox would have *chalent* [a special dish made with beef, beans, or potatoes] because it was cooked on Friday overnight, and it was still warm when I brought it home from the bakery at twelve or one on Saturday afternoon. My mother made the chalent in a big cast-iron pot, and I took it to the bakery on Fridays, and they baked it in the oven. Even as a small boy, I went to the bakery on Saturday afternoon and brought home the chalent. The pot was so heavy I had to put a towel between the two handles, which looked like ears, to carry it home. There was always a brown bag over it, and on the way home, I took out a potato and ate it.

There is an incident I will never forget about a very large family that was very poor. The father was a *trager*. He picked up and carried heavy packages on his back to deliver to stores or families. One time one of his children by mistake picked up our chalent instead of their own. When I got to the bakery there was only one pot of chalent left, so I took it home. When I got home, you should have seen my mother's eyes. The chalent was not like ours at all! Mother used to clean out the big cow intestines and stuff them with seasoned flour and rendered pieces of poultry skin, which she put between the potatoes. It was very delicious. But the chalent I picked up that day was not fit to eat. My mother said, "Let them have ours. Wait until they are finished, but then I want my pot back." We did not eat their chalent. Later, I took their chalent, still in their pot, back and said, "I want our cast-iron pot back." They were embarrassed, but I said, "Don't worry about it." Then their mother said that they had enjoyed the chalent, so I took our pot and came back home. That was my mother—she was a good woman.

Sometimes we did not have chalent. We ate leftovers from Sabbath dinner. On Saturday afternoon my father would listen to me read my Hebrew lessons. I used to read and translate. I always tried to sneak away while my father was sleeping on Saturday afternoon. I would say, "You were sleeping, and you could not listen to me." Sometimes I knew the lessons, and sometimes I didn't.

Sometimes on Saturday afternoons in the summer, we went to the river Warta, swam, and played on the beach. I remember the Hasidim were so mad. They asked Rabbi Lipshitz, "How can they go swimming? How can they go to a *Hechalutz* club meeting?" The Hechalutz and the *Hapoel* [Zionist organizations] used to be in the same building. We used to go over there and sing, play Ping-Pong, and dance the *hora*.

Rabbi Lipshitz was a very, very smart man. He said, "I can do nothing about it. If I tell them, they are not going to listen to me anyway. They are going to do what they want. So as long as they come Saturday mornings to shul, I cannot help it."

4

The Non-Jewish Community

KONIN, POLAND, 1925–1939. The Jewish community and the non-Jewish community dealt with each other on a daily basis. Many Jews were shopkeepers and tradesmen. The baker was Jewish, and I'm sure that on Sabbath he had a *Shabbas Goy* (the term we used for a non-Jewish person who would do needed chores that we could not do on the Sabbath) to take out the chalent. Jews were not supposed to do any kind of work on the Sabbath. The Polish people worked in the city, sometimes as janitors in Jewish homes, like in our apartment building, or they had little farms.

Most of the farms in Poland belonged to Christians, but some Jews owned farms and were farmers. Most of the Jews were merchants, storekeepers, tailors, or shoemakers. Few Jews were professionals like bankers, doctors, dentists, or lawyers. Many years ago in Poland, Jews could not own land, and they could not get a higher education. There were a very few rich Jews in Poland. We had some Jewish doctors and dentists in our city. But you never saw a Jewish person build a house.

Some Polish people in Konin were educated, and some were not. The educators were well respected. Being a kid and looking back, we didn't bother them, and they didn't bother us. As a little boy, my world was Konin, and I figure that I would have stayed there, gotten married, and had children.

In the summers, the days were long. We played stickball in the streets. We also played soccer in the sand, and it was hard to run through that sand. I organized the soccer team. I was always the organizer. Everybody used to get a groszy or two from their parents, and we saved our money. Our first soccer ball was made from old socks and material. Finally, we pooled our money together and bought a leather soccer ball. We treated that ball like a baby. The ball had a bladder, and we cleaned and oiled the ball regularly. We made it shine and kept it soft. We played barefoot because we did not dare play in our shoes. If you got your shoes scratched or knocked off the sole and then came home, you were going to get the biggest spanking of your life. We also used to run around the blocks and play hide-and-seek on the third or fourth floor and in the attics. I used to climb a steep roof, and they could not find me. It was fun. I was always taking chances.

We had a movie house that showed American and English movies, but who could afford to go to the movies? I could not afford the twenty or thirty groszy. I used to sneak in through a small window and hoped I wouldn't get caught. But if they caught me, they threw me out. We also had a Yiddish drama group that performed plays in Yiddish in Konin. I used to earn a few groszy going around and distributing their leaflets. My sister Ester was involved in acting with the theater.

In 1936 and 1937, we were aware of what was going on in Germany. We knew that all the Polish citizens living there were being sent back to Poland. We always spoke of leaving and going to Palestine [now Israel], but we never had a chance. The English, who ruled Palestine at the time, had a Jewish quota, and they said, if you are learning to be a farmer, we will let you in. My older brother Szlama, before he was drafted into the army, was planning to go to a *kibbutz* [cooperative farm] to learn farming for six months outside Lublin, on the northeastern side of Poland. However, after he was drafted, he could not leave Poland. The war broke out, and he could have still gone if they could have gotten enough visas, but he didn't make it. There were lots of people in that kibbutz, and we had one in our city, too. People came there to train for migrating to what was then Palestine. They wanted to get away from very poor families. On a kibbutz they could get work. The city would help them find a job, and all the money they earned went to one pot. They did not have to worry about where to sleep, and they had enough food to eat. They also trained for agriculture to immigrate to Palestine.

My brothers Avram and Szlama were in the army for two years. Szlama was a machine gunner. When the war broke out, Szlama was fighting against the Germans, and he was captured in Warsaw when Poland fell to the enemy. When Warsaw signed the surrender, Szlama was helping defend Warsaw. The Nazis captured the Polish soldiers and took them as prisoners of war to a camp not too far from Warsaw. The Nazis told the soldiers that if they surrendered, they could go home. Some of them were sent to Germany to a labor camp, but Szlama came home to be with the family. We were together until we were deported.

Part II

The War Years and Post-War Years in Germany

– 5 –

It Was a Miracle

KONIN, POLAND, SEPTEMBER 1939. At the end of World War I, Poland became a republic again, after being under Russian and German rule. Poland was very rich in agriculture, and life was good. However, in 1933 the Nazis took over Germany with the selection of Adolph Hitler to lead the country. By 1938 war clouds were gathering. The Nazis had marched into the Sudetenland, part of Czechoslovakia, with the consent of Prime Minister Chamberlain of England. They invaded Poland on September 1, 1939. Konin being so close to the German border, it was among the first Polish cities to be invaded.

I was fourteen years old when the Nazis marched into our city, Konin. That was the day they broke into our synagogue during the *Rosh Hashanah* [Jewish New Year] service. I remember like it was yesterday. Two of my brothers and I sang together in the choir. I loved singing in the choir on the High Holidays. We all dressed in our new best clothes. The service was long, but we prayed with feeling and added to the spiritual mood of the service. I still remember which prayer we were singing that morning. It was the part about whether or not God writes your name in the Book of Life for the coming new year. I had no idea how true that prayer would become.

The Nazis burst in, yelling for everyone to get out and go

home. All of us ran out of the shul except the extremely religious
Hasidim, who had a room adjacent to the main synagogue, and
stayed and prayed. A little later, looking out my window from
home, I saw the Hasidim running home. They still had their
prayer shawls on. Those Hasidim were lucky they weren't killed.

Several days later, the Nazis gathered up some Jews in the
town of Konin. Some of the Jews of our community were ordered
back into the synagogue and house of learning to bring outside
all the religious articles. Prayer books, prayer shawls, special
high velvet hats worn by the choir on the High Holidays, and
our holiest scrolls, the Torah, containing the Five books of
Moses, were taken out. These holy items were piled high in one
of our smaller town squares, which was close to the shul and in
the heart of the Jewish neighborhood, called the *Tepper Marik,* as
it was also the "market square." It was a lively market area where
all the shops belonged to Jews and the farmers would bring their
goods on Tuesdays and Fridays.

When no one was looking, I ran back into the synagogue and
grabbed my *talis* [prayer shawl] and choir hat. I put them under
my shirt and walked out, feeling good that I saved these precious
items. I took my hat and prayer shawl right home and gave them
to my father. He kept the hat and talis with him at all times. I'm
sure my father took them with him to Treblinka, the death camp.

When the Jews had finished piling the Torah, prayer books,
and other items in one of the smaller squares that was close to
the shul, the Nazis tried to make our rabbi, Rabbi Lipschitz, put
a match to the pile. The rabbi wouldn't do it. I was told the rabbi
said, "I'd rather die than put a match to the Holy items."

Finally, an SS man put the match to the books, scrolls, and
shawls. I'm not sure if the Nazis put some gasoline on the pile to
make it burn or not. I do know that as soon as that pile started
burning, it started raining. Not a heavy rain, but a steady rain.
That pile burned for three days and three nights. The sky rained
for three days and three nights. The more that pile burned, the
more the sky rained. When it stopped burning, it stopped raining. I think it was a miracle! Somebody upstairs must have been
crying over the loss of those precious items.

There was a lot of smoke, because the Torah never really
did catch fire, being made of parchment. It just got scorched.

The prayer books were badly burned. On the fourth day, I went and got my friend Nachmusz, whose family still had a horse and wagon. I talked him into hitching up the horse and wagon and driving with me to the square to gather up the Torah, prayer books, and ashes to be loaded on the wagon and take them to the cemetery. In the Jewish tradition, these items must be properly buried when they are torn or "worn out."

As we loaded the wagon, an SS officer came over and asked, "What are you doing over here?"

Quickly, I said in my broken German, as I was able to do because we spoke Yiddish at home, which was close to German, "We are cleaning up the street. We are taking this trash to the River Warta and throwing it in."

He must have believed me, because he let us finish loading the religious items and ashes. We headed in the direction of the River Warta. As soon as we were out of sight of the SS officer, we turned and went to the cemetery.

On the way, we stopped and picked up a man—I don't remember his name. He was a *shomer,* the man who would sit with the dead bodies until they were buried. In Judaism, once a person dies, their body is never left alone until the burial. This ritual is done to make sure that no harm comes to the dead person, since the person is no longer able to take care of himself.

The three of us dug a grave just inside the cemetery wall. Because the cemetery is consecrated ground, and because these religious items were destroyed or "died" in an unnatural way, Jewish law does not allow them to be buried in the middle of the cemetery proper. We finished digging the grave and buried all those precious items. I was so sad. We said *Kaddish,* the Jewish prayer for the dead. We got out of there as fast as we could, horse, wagon, and all.

Watching us the whole time doing all this was the cemetery caretaker. We found out later that he was a *Volksdeutscher,* someone born in Poland of German descent. He knew we were not supposed to be burying those items. He ran and told the SS what we had done. The SS looked for us, but by the time he got back to the cemetery with the Nazis, we had buried everything and were nowhere to be found.

6

The Bullet Holes Are Still in the Wall

KONIN, POLAND, OCTOBER 1939. Life was never the same after the Nazis invaded Konin. Things I had taken for granted—going to school, playing with anyone I wanted, roaming all over town whenever I pleased—all taken away, all gone. Life changed for me forever that year. Some friends who were Volksdeutcher, of German parentage, put on swastika armbands and said, "We don't play with Jews anymore." There were also some Polish friends who did not want to play with me. Everything I had known, everything I had loved, all that was precious to me, disappeared.

Each day the Nazis issued new rules. First, they imposed a curfew: No Jews were allowed to leave their homes from 6:00 P.M. to 6:00 A.M. Non-Jews were not allowed to leave their homes from 9:00 P.M. until 6:00 A.M. Then, Jewish kids were not allowed in school. Jews were not allowed to go to synagogue. The Nazis made a horse stable out of our synagogue. The Nazis forcefully took non-Jewish and Jewish hostages and put them in jail.

I remember the first time the Nazis killed people in our town. The German Nazi in charge of our town said, "If anything happens to a German, all the hostages will be killed." The Nazis began a slow process of taking away our rights, our freedom, and some of our belongings, such as radios and fur coats.

Ten days after the Nazis came, on *Yom Kippur*, the holiest day in the Jewish year, the call went out for everyone to go to the big town square. Nobody wanted to go. Everyone was afraid. I was excited; I thought I was going to listen to the orchestra. When I came to the large city square, I saw only a few non-Jews, some of whom were farmers.

Our city had two squares because farmers came to town during the weekdays to sell their farm products, such as chickens, eggs, butter, and vegetables. They gathered in these squares.

Seven Nazis brought out two of the hostages, one Jew, Mr. Slotki, and one non-Jew, Mr. Kurowski. The hostages were marched and made to stand in front of a building wall. I waited for the hostages to say something about what was going on. Nobody said anything.

Suddenly, the six SS soldiers marched with their leader and stood right in front of me, facing the hostages, who they put standing close to the wall and facing the people the Nazis had ordered to come to the square. The leader offered the hostages handkerchiefs as blindfolds, which they refused to use. He then said something to his men I couldn't hear. The leader stepped to the side and gave his men orders to shoot the hostages. Shots rang out. Both men fell to the pavement. This was the first time I ever saw people shot and bleeding to death. The bullet holes in the wall are still there today, and a memorial stone has been placed on the wall near them. Can you imagine?

I ran home, so fast I thought my feet would come off. I told my family and neighbors what I saw. At first nobody could believe what I said. Later, the neighbors said that the men held as hostages had done nothing wrong, the men hadn't done anything to deserve being killed.

Several days afterward, the Nazis rounded up all the non-Jewish teachers from Konin and the vicinity. When I looked out of my window, I saw teachers from my school. All of those teachers were marching with SS men in front of and behind them. The SS men marched the teachers to the Jewish cemetery and shot everyone. They were 100 percent non-Jewish teachers. The

Nazis rounded them up, took them out, and shot them, one by one, through the head with their guns in the field. There is still a memorial in Konin now, put up in their memory. All were killed in one afternoon.

Why did they kill the teachers? I think it was because this was basically a small community in which most people had maybe a fifth-grade education. The people most likely to fight against the Nazis were the people who had the most education, the teachers. By killing the teachers, the Nazis prevented anyone from speaking out against what they were doing to people.

After the teachers were killed, I think there was more fear in the people's homes. At 6:00 at night, all the windows were drawn because everybody was looking out at what was going on outside.

We had to change our way of life, our way of doing things, once the Nazis arrived. Before the Nazis came, we had a town *shochet* [ritual slaughterer] who butchered our beef and poultry in a special and painless way so that the dietary laws of *kasherut* [properly preparing foods to be kosher] were observed. Once the Nazis came, our shochet was afraid to do the ritual slaughtering, because it was not allowed. *Succoth* was coming up, and my mother wanted a chicken for the holiday dinner. We were not supposed to eat a chicken unless it was killed in this certain way.

I decided to go to Golina, a small town about ten kilometers [six miles] away. Since it was really a village, I thought the shochet might still be butchering. I had a plan. I put on torn pants and a shirt. I took a bicycle, put a basket on the back with a couple of chickens in it, and began pedaling to Golina. I wasn't too worried about getting caught, because I didn't look Jewish. I had blond hair, blue eyes, and spoke Polish pretty well, so people who didn't know me thought I was Polish.

I made up a story for what I would tell the SS or the *Gestapo* officers if they stopped me. I decided if the SS or Gestapo stopped me, I would tell them, "Look, those chickens are poisonous, so I killed them to take to the Jews so they could eat them and get sick." I figured it was a good story to use when I got stopped. I never did get stopped. Lots of soldiers were on the road, and nobody paid any attention to me.

By the time I made it back to Konin, it was already 6:00 at

night. My whole neighborhood heard me pedaling like crazy up those streets made of rounded rocks. The noise from my bicycle on those stones must have sounded like a herd of elephants. My brothers opened our front door, and I jumped off the bicycle and ran into the house. My parents both took deep breaths and sighed with relief that I was finally home. What a holiday that was with the kosher chickens for my family to eat!

7

Don't You Worry About Tomorrow

KONIN, POLAND, NOVEMBER 1939. Before the Nazis came to Konin, my family was the center of my world. My parents, my brothers and sisters, they meant everything to me. My happiest memories are of sitting with my family after a meal, singing songs, laughing and joking.

After the Nazis came to town, everything changed. We could feel the Nazis all around us. They marched everywhere; we could hear them blocks away. Their boots had nails in the heels and soles. Those nails made a tremendous noise when hitting the rocks our streets were made of.

Whenever we heard the Nazis approaching, we were especially afraid for my two sisters, whom we rushed into the basement. The Nazis were known for taking young girls and women from their houses and abusing them. We had a trap door in the floor with a rug over it leading into the basement. When we heard the sounds of the soldiers approaching, we pulled up that rug, hurried my sisters through the trap door, pulled the rug up over the basement door, and set the table on top of everything. Once the Nazis passed our house, my sisters could come out again until the next time.

My mother was a little bit of a visionary. She often had an intuition about things that were going to happen before they actually happened. One day, soon after the two hostages were shot to death in the town square, she looked at me with sad eyes and said, "Mendel, one day we are going to part. You are going to go your way, and I am going to go my way."

I said, "Mother, what are you talking about? We will always be together—what is this?" I didn't understand what she was trying to tell me.

She kept talking as if she hadn't heard me. "When you are by yourself, walking down the street, suppose a man comes up to you. This man says, 'If I don't have something to eat, I am going to die.' What would you do?" she asked me.

"Mother, if he is going to die, there is nothing I can do about it," I said.

She asked, "Do you have a penny in your pocket?"

"Yes," I said.

"Give it to him," my mother told me.

"How can I give away my last penny?" I asked her. "Tomorrow I have to buy bread for myself with this penny."

"Give him the penny," my mother told me again. "With this penny, you are saving a life today. Don't you worry about tomorrow."

She looked at me again with sad eyes and said, "I am not worrying about you, Mendel. When they throw you in the fire, you will always walk out from it." That stuck in my head. It took me years and years to finally understand what my mother was trying to tell me that day.

Mother taught me to never give up my hope and my belief. Everything I went through during the war, I always thought positively that I would survive, no matter what happened. Those three things, hope, belief, and positive thinking, are what kept me alive for the next five and a half years.

Two months had passed since the Nazis took over our town, and we tried to continue life as normally as we could. There were little changes all around, almost too small to notice. It seemed like a dark cloud descended over Konin. Everything was so quiet, because people were so afraid.

Soon, the German Nazis began coming around to the middle of the small square each morning with big trucks. They would go from house to house, rounding up Jews, loading them onto their trucks, and taking the Jews to go out to work for them at different jobs. The Jews were forced to scrub potatoes, clean floors, and generally take care of the German soldiers in the city. The Jews never got paid for what they did. Essentially, the Jews worked for the German army as free labor.

One day in late November, the Nazis came into our home and told us we had five to ten minutes to get out of our house. We were in a state of complete surprise. I can't remember what we took. We all grabbed a few belongings, whatever we could carry. Some clothes, blankets, and some food. My whole family, my parents, three brothers, two sisters, and I, went to the square. Most of my relatives were already gathered there. The Nazis took us into a building on the outskirts of town that had been a Polish military school.

Once in the building, the SS told everyone to bring their jewelry and other valuables to a table in the front for safekeeping. The SS said we would get a receipt for our belongings, and the items would be returned to us upon our arrival at our new destination. I didn't like the sound of this at all. I told my parents, "We are not going to give them anything. Do not give them anything. We will hide our valuables ourselves." Lots of people did go up to the front and gave them jewelry and money, but we didn't.

My brothers were tailors and made all our clothes. Of course, in those days, everybody had handmade clothes. My brothers had sewn hidden pockets into some of our clothes' linings. My mother had lots of jewelry, which she wore on special occasions and holidays. She had brought her jewelry with her, but had hidden it in the special lining my brothers made. Her beautiful rings, bracelets, chains, and diamonds, were all tucked away in secret pockets.

I took two of the rings from my mother and went over to the Ukrainian guard assigned to watch us. I gave the guard the two rings, as a deposit, telling him I would be back. I told him, "Now when I come back, you be here to let me back in the building." I had to get out of the building to see what was going on, what they were planning for us.

Once outside in the streets, everything was quiet. Nothing moved; silence. There was nothing going on. Most of the Jews had been taken to the school, and the non-Jews were keeping out of sight. I thought about going back home, but decided not to. When I got back to that school, the Ukrainian guard was nowhere to be found. Neither were the rings. I never saw the rings or that guard again.

8

Being With My Family, Transport to Ostrowiec

We waited in that building until nightfall, when the Nazis lined us up. We walked to the railroad station, where empty railroad cattle boxcars were waiting. These boxcars were built for twelve cows. The Nazis packed between 75 and 100 people in each boxcar.

I was lucky—my family and I were all loaded in the same boxcar. Lots of my relatives were also in the boxcar with us. Some of the children were separated from their parents, put on the same train, but in different cars. I was lucky, being together with my family. There we were, packed in like herrings, destination unknown. At least herrings are packed in water; we were jammed in without food or water.

This tiny wooden boxcar became our living room, dining room, bathroom, and cemetery. We were packed so tightly, when someone died, we stacked their body against the wall so the rest of us had more room to breathe.

We traveled that way for three days and three nights. Sometimes during the day, one of my relatives would lift me up to look out the little window with the barbed wire around it. I called out the names of the cities I saw as we passed. This way, we were able to tell which direction we were going. Finally, we came to Warsaw. I am sure it was not a direct route, because it took so many days.

We pulled into the Warsaw station and stayed all day while the SS and the mayor of Warsaw met to decide whether or not to take us into the ghetto. After waiting all day with no one allowed on or off the train, the mayor must have decided that Warsaw already had too many Jews in the ghetto, and he would not take us. The train started moving on again without anyone getting off.

We left Warsaw and continued traveling down to the southeastern part of Poland. I remember people were pretty quiet by this time, not much discussion was going on. I was a kid, so I didn't pay too much attention, but I think the people were really, really down. Maybe the parents knew what was going on, but did not want to talk about it because of the children, I'm not sure. My parents told us everything was going to be fine, and we were going to a new city to begin a new life.

After three days and three nights of train riding, with no food, no water, no room to lay down to sleep, we finally reached the town of Ostrowiec. The *Judenrat* [Jewish Council] decided to accept us; I don't think they really had any other choice. We were taken to a big school, and the Jewish community brought us some food—soup and bread. Then the Jewish community leaders came and assigned housing. Christians did not have to move outside the ghetto once it was established, and Jews already living there remained in their homes.

My family was assigned to a home near the ghetto outskirts. Sixteen of us were assigned to two rooms in the upstairs of a house, very small, like an attic. Besides the eight in my family, my aunt, uncle, their two daughters, and another family also lived in these two rooms. I remember the slanted ceiling. During the day, we put a panel of wood across two wooden sawhorses to make a table. At night, we put the wooden panel on the bedposts, making a two-layer bed. Those two rooms were so small that some of us had to sleep on the floor.

9

I Never Stole Anything

OSTROWIEC, POLAND, FEBRUARY 1940. Once we were settled in the Ostrowiec ghetto, everyone except the very young and the very old were required to work. Life here was very different than in Konin. In Konin we had to observe curfews, but still kept some of our freedom. In Ostrowiec, all that changed.

We were not allowed to leave the ghetto, unless on a work detail accompanied by guards. No walls or barbed wire surrounded the ghetto, but there were certain streets and buildings that were boundaries we were not supposed to cross. Even though we weren't supposed to leave the ghetto, some people would sneak out. Now, this was tricky, because the SS and German police constantly patrolled on motorcycles and bicycles, looking for Jews outside the ghetto. When a Jew was found outside the ghetto, he or she was immediately shot.

A short time after we were resettled in the Ostrowiec ghetto, my sister Ester and Wolf Kaczka, who were engaged, decided to get married in the ghetto. When a Jewish neighbor found out they wanted to get married, he and his family opened their home to them and arranged a beautiful wedding. Our family and relatives attended. Everyone was happy!

In the ghetto, there was no school for me to attend. Since I was now fifteen and small for my age, I was not required to go to work. I spent my days sneaking out of the ghetto in the morning and back in at night. I did this easily since I didn't look Jewish.

Taking pants, jackets, and coats my brothers made, I sold and traded these to Polish farmers. I bought or traded for eggs, butter, potatoes, flour, and bread from different people. The farmers never suspected I was Jewish, either. If they had known, they would have charged me a premium for the goods, or simply turned me over to the Nazis. At this time, food was very hard to find and get in the ghetto, and this was a way for me to do my part to feed my family.

Even though I was not supposed to work, I went around the ghetto to find things I could do to help my family and relatives. One thing I must mention is that I never STOLE anything. Stealing is a dirty word. "Organizing" is much more sophisticated. I found lots of ways to organize and make money, even when living in the ghetto.

My brothers, who were tailors, made me a very long coat with very large pockets. These were not actually pockets at all, but fake pockets cut through to the inner lining of the coat fabric. So, when I filled up my pockets, I actually filled the entire bottom of my coat. It was almost impossible to tell there was anything at the bottom. My brothers also made me a pair of pants with very wide legs, but which fit very tightly around my ankles. I wore these when volunteering to clean things up for the Germans outside the ghetto.

The Germans never seemed to mind having someone else do their cleaning for them—anything to keep from having to do it themselves. The Nazis were glad to have extra help doing things they didn't want to do. The Germans thought I was just some little Polish kid out looking to make some money. I just kept my eyes open and offered to help.

One day I went to the sugar factory, where the made sugar from sugar beets, which grew in Poland. Looking like a little Polish kid with my torn pants and blond hair, I slipped by the security guard along with the workers as they walked in a line through the little guardhouse. As I worked unloading sugar beets, I'd put some sugar in some little bags that I had in my pocket and took it home. I only worked there a few days, but this too was a help to my family.

There was a nearby bakery where the German soldiers would come with covered wagons to get bread for the troops. I loaded the bread while the Germans sat in the front of the wagon, talking and laughing. The Germans were counting the bread; I also counted the loaves for myself. As I loaded the bread on the wagon, I put loaves of bread in between the wagon box and the ropes that held the wagon cover down.

When the German soldiers were not watching, I slipped the loaves out and put them into my big coat. I could get three or four loaves this way to take home and share with my family. There was this little old Polish lady who lived above the bakery. She owned the bakery before it was taken over by the Nazis. She watched from her window as I took the bread; I can still see her today. She used to tell me, "When they catch you taking the bread, they are going to kill you."

I looked back at her and said, "I'm not worried about it."

I guess being fifteen helped me in some ways. Teenagers don't think about dying. I kept focused on what I could do to help my family and relatives, how I could bring in food or money. Each of us in the family did our part to survive in the ghetto. My oldest brother, Avram, was supposed to go to work every day, but he did not. He worked at home doing his tailoring, and my father went to the work detail for the Nazis in his place.

As my father was in his sixties, he was not required to join the work detail, but he went instead of Avram. One day my father did not go to work. An SS officer came to arrest Avram, because he had not reported to work. The officer was going to put my brother in jail. I walked over to the SS officer and said, "Why are you taking him to jail? I'll go to jail instead." It didn't matter to the SS officer who went to jail, just as long as somebody did. The SS officer was just doing his "duty," so they took me to jail in place of my brother. Can you imagine a fifteen-year-old boy going to jail?

The Ostrowiec jail is still standing today. It's nothing like the jails here in the United States. The jail cells were in the basement of this building. After we used the latrine, which was a bucket in the corner of our jail cell, we had to clean up everything by hand. The smell was terrible. There was water running down the walls. I was so cold in that jail.

I was in a cell with another guy. I don't know what kind of crime he committed. I guess he liked me right away, because he didn't bother me. Maybe it was because I was young. We used to go outside in the jail courtyard for some fresh air and exercise. Other prisoners would ask me what cell I was in. "I'm in the cell with him," I told them, pointing to my cellmate.

The other prisoners shook their heads and said, "Oh my God."

I was never sure why they put me in the cell with this guy, but he never bothered me, so I didn't care.

There was a small window at the top of our cell, level with the street. I would look out and see my mother walking up and down the sidewalk. I am sure she was thinking what would happen to her little son in jail. Since I was the youngest of her six children and her baby, I'm sure she worried about me constantly. It was horrible, and they put me, a fifteen-year-old boy, in the same cell with a criminal.

One afternoon, we were walking outside in the courtyard for our usual exercise. I overheard the guards saying that the next day they were going to liquidate the people in the jail. I thought, "Uh-oh, and I'm only a young boy." I quickly walked over to the front gate being guarded by a German soldier.

The soldier stopped me and asked, "Where are you going?"

"I'm supposed to walk through the next gate," I said. I told him I had gotten into the jail accidentally.

The German guard looked at me and saw a little Polish kid who had no business being in jail. "Get out and get away!" he ordered, opening the gate for me. I did not hesitate. I walked away toward the next gate and was out. I was free!

The very next day, all of the inmates of the entire jail were taken out and shot. Somebody upstairs was looking over me to see that I would survive to tell the story.

– 10 –

I Was Never Still Very Long

OSTROWIEC, POLAND, MARCH 1940. The Germans continued bringing people into the Ostrowiec ghetto. There were just too many people and not enough food. The conditions were so unsanitary. We had a tremendous epidemic of typhus, both head and stomach. The Judenrat took over a building and made it into a hospital, with Jewish doctors taking care of the patients. One day, I overheard some of the doctors saying if they just had some oranges they could save the lives of the typhus patients.

Ostrowiec had a brewery where I used to watch Germans unloading oranges and putting them in the basement. The top of the basement wall had a small window opening up onto the street level. I remembered the doctors talking about those oranges, and I decided to go to the brewery and see if I could stick my head through that basement window. I figured if I could get my head through that little opening, the rest of my body would fit through, too.

I was wearing the coat my brother made for me, with the false pockets sewn into the lining and at the bottom. I worked my way through that little opening and filled my coat with oranges so that I could barely walk. Putting the oranges in my pockets, they soon filled the bottom of my coat. Now I had a problem—I couldn't fit through the window anymore. There was really nothing left for me to do except open the door to the brewery basement and walk out, and so I did. I went home, left a few oranges for my family, and put the rest in a basket to take to the hospital.

I got to the hospital and told one of the doctors, "I have oranges for you to use."

The doctor looked puzzled when I gave him the oranges and asked, "Where did you get these from?"

I told him, "What's the difference where I got the oranges? I have them in the basket and you need them."

He asked me how much I wanted for the oranges.

I told him, "Not a penny. They are to help the typhus people." I didn't know it then, but the reason for the oranges was their Vitamin C.

I was never still for very long in the ghetto. I was always going to farms and factories, looking for ways to volunteer so that I could keep organizing food for my family. I was able to go places and get away with a lot of things because I didn't look Jewish. Nobody would ever know I was Jewish unless someone "pointed the finger" at me.

There was a slaughterhouse outside the ghetto where I would go and carry beef to the soldiers' trucks. The beef was cut into quarters, and the soldiers were happy to let me carry it so they wouldn't get their clothes dirty. I guess the beef was sent to soldiers on the front lines. Those beef quarters were so heavy. In the wintertime, the beef would freeze, and I could easily tear the fat off.

When the soldiers weren't looking, I would tear off the fat and throw it over the fence to my brother Reuven, who was waiting on the other side. Reuven gathered the fat and took it home to my mother, who used it for cooking and making soap. I remember she used it to make *greeven* for us to eat—it was so good!

Across the city, a German butcher had a smokehouse where he made salami and ring salami. I would go there and help grind the meat, mix in spices, and stuff it into cow intestines. We tied the intestines into links and took them to his basement to be smoked. The butcher also smoked hams, but I was more interested in the salamis so my family would have something to eat.

When no one was looking, I put some salami rings up my pants legs in the large, oversized pants my brother made for me. Those ringed salamis wrapped around my legs made me walk funny. Usually, the Nazis never noticed, but one day one of them asked, "What happened to you?" I told him I was a little tired and went home.

Life in the Ostrowiec ghetto was very difficult, and everyone did whatever they could to earn a little bit of money. There was a soda factory in the ghetto belonging to a non-Jew. Mr. Green, whom I knew from Konin, worked for him. Mr. Green had his own soda factory in Konin and made different flavored sodas, along with carbonated water. I particularly remember his delicious orange soda. I decided to take soft drinks outside the ghetto and sell them to the stores and farmers.

My father, brothers, and I found an old wagon axle with two wheels. Using lumber lying around the ghetto, we made a box and fastened it to the axle. We attached two long two-by-fours to the side of the box and placed another board across the two-by-fours so I could push the cart with my stomach. Then we loaded the little pushcart up with many bottles of soft drinks and a big block of ice. When I sold soft drinks, I had to give them ice, too. That cart was so heavy when it was full that I not only had to push it with my stomach, but my father and brother had to come help me push it up the little hill.

I made pretty good money selling those sodas outside the ghetto to the Polish stores and farmers. At the farmhouses, I would exchange sodas for eggs, butter, and other food. Using the money I made from the sodas, I would buy bread and flour for my family. Sometimes people would give me a piece of bread and margarine or salami; these I would take home to share with my family. I hid all these goods under the bottles and straw so that if anybody stopped me, all they would find were the bottles and nothing else.

I remember that summer seeing soldiers in the field just outside the ghetto, stopping to rest before going to the Russian front. I decided to start selling sodas to the soldiers. There was one officer in charge of the soldiers going to the front. When I asked him if I could sell the sodas, I told him, "For you, the soda is free." Then I would give him a cold drink. I figured it was good business to always give the officer a free soft drink.

One day I was out selling the soft drinks and doing so well, I hated to leave. I had sold out, so my father and brother loaded up another pushcart for me and brought more sodas so that I could sell them, too. My father, with his blond hair, didn't look Jewish. My brother Szlama was a brunette and did look Jewish, so when they brought me the sodas, my brother stayed on the ghetto side of the street.

I never could understand why a German could never tell a Jew from a non-Jew. It was always the Polish people pointing out a Jewish person. The only way the Poles could identify Jews was by the Yiddish expressions they used, since Yiddish was the first language spoken at home.

This particular day, a Polish mother and her son were also out selling soft drinks to the soldiers. When the woman saw my father and brother bringing me more sodas, she started yelling, "*Jude, Jude!*" [Jew, Jew]. All of a sudden, I saw a big group of soldiers gathering around my father and brother. I thought, "Uh-oh, they are in trouble now." I went over to where everyone was standing and said in my best German, "What is going on over here?"

The German officer, the one I gave free soft drinks to, told me, "This woman is saying these people are Jewish."

Knowing I had to say something to save my brother and father, I quickly said, "What are you talking about, that they are Jewish?" I pointed to the woman. "You know why she is saying they are Jewish?" I told the officer, "She is saying these men are Jewish because she is afraid they're going to tell you that *she* is Jewish!"

The German officer looked at me and said, "Are you sure?" I said, "Yes."

Finally he said, "Okay, take them to the SS headquarters."

The Germans took the lady and her son across the street to the Gestapo headquarters. I turned to my father and brother and said, "You go. Take off! Leave everything and just go!" They left very quickly, leaving the pushcart with all the extra soft drinks they brought. I left, too, and didn't bother to take the empty bottles because I knew we didn't have much time to get away. I knew nothing would happen to the woman and her son, because they could prove they were Polish by their identity papers.

The next day I went back to the field to collect the bottles we left. I had put a deposit on them and didn't want to lose it. I saw the same woman and her son. She, too, had come back to get her bottles, most of which were still full, left behind when they were taken by the SS to be questioned.

I looked at her and asked, "How was it?"

She still didn't know I was Jewish. She looked at me and asked, "Why did you say we were Jewish?"

I looked her right in the eyes, saying, "You ought to be ashamed of yourself. The only thing I could do to save those Jews was to say *you* were Jewish. I knew the Gestapo was not going to do anything to you. You could prove you were not Jewish, right? You were free after about an hour, weren't you?"

"Yes," she said.

I continued, "You better be ashamed. What would you have gained if those people had been killed?"

She didn't say anything back to me. After that, I did not see her selling soft drinks anymore.

Things kept getting worse for us in the ghetto. I remember one Gestapo man who had a trained white German Shepherd dog. He would walk up and down the street, holding the dog on a leash. All of a sudden, the Gestapo guard would yell, "*Jude!*" and the dog would jump on the Jew, ripping him apart until the Gestapo called the dog off. The person bled to death. Many times, the dog would jump on the person's throat. The Gestapo trained the dogs to kill Jews.

When my sister Ryfka found out that the Nazis had surrounded the ghetto, she decided to come and stay with us. Ryfka, who was blond, did not look Jewish and spoke good Polish. She was able to stay with Christian neighbors, since she and their daughter had become good friends. We begged her to leave and stay with her friend, but she no longer wanted to. She decided to stay with the family.

11

Mendel, You Have to Be Strong

LEAVING OSTROWIEC, POLAND, FALL 1942. My family lived in the Ostrowiec ghetto for three years. On October 11, 1942, the Gestapo again came into our home and told us we had to leave, that we were going to be resettled. My family grabbed a few belongings and walked out of our house together. As we were walking to the big town square, I looked to my left and saw the SS selecting people. I didn't know what the SS were doing, but I said to my brother Reuven, "Come on, let's go over there where the Nazis are selecting people."

Reuven didn't want to go with me. He said, "No, I want to stay with the family." He just stood there, but I pulled on his arm and made him come. "Don't worry," I said, "When we find out where the family went, we can always follow them." To this day, I cannot tell you why I wanted to go over to where the Nazis were selecting people. Maybe it was instinct, but something told me not to stay with the family. I told Reuven, "Come on, we'll catch up with the family later."

I waved to my parents. I don't know if they saw me wave, because they were walking toward the big square with a lot of other people. I didn't know what was going to happen to them.

At first, I thought we were all going to be resettled to another city, and everything would be okay.

Reuven and I went toward the area, which was the small square, where the Nazis were selecting people. The Nazis let Reuven through because he was tall and five years older than I was. They pushed me back because I was skinny and short—I guess they thought I wouldn't be any good for them. I still didn't know what the selection was all about, but I knew I wanted to be with my brother. I waited until the guards were distracted and sneaked through to the other side, where I found Reuven in the small square.

Nightfall came, and we were taken out of that small square. As we walked past the large square where the rest of my family and relatives had assembled, the square was completely empty. Everyone was gone. We were taken to a small ghetto that had been made that day. I always wondered how they could build a wall so quickly around that small ghetto. A wooden fence, built in only one day, surrounded the entire ghetto. We were put in small rooms with bunks.

I was in a room with my brother. Looking back, I know I was crying, because I was very lonesome for the rest of my family. I cried the whole night. I was sixteen years old, and I didn't know where they were. I had Reuven, but my other brothers, sisters, and parents were gone. I had a feeling I would not see them anymore. When a person loses a loved one, you know when they die, and you know they are dead. I had a feeling I that I was not going to see my brothers, my father, my mother, and my sisters. I wasn't going to see them anymore, and I had to go on every day of my life. I had to fight for survival. I couldn't think about them, I couldn't worry anymore, because if I started to worry and think about them, I would be gone.

That was the last time I was crying. Finally, I pulled myself together and said, "Mendel, you have to be strong." I knew I was alone now, but I never gave up my hope and belief. I was always positive that I would survive.

During this time, I was able to get false identification papers with my name reported as Marjan Jakubowski.

We had stayed in that small ghetto about two weeks when Reuven decided he didn't want to stay there any longer. He decided to go join the Jewish underground resistance fighters. I begged him not to go with this underground. "Reuven," I said, "don't go—it's no good. It's not the right thing to do." Once again, I felt that something was going to go wrong.

Reuven wouldn't listen to me. "It is better that I go with them to fight and die fighting than to sit over here and do nothing," he said.

We had heard that there were Jewish and non-Jewish partisans hiding in the forest outside the ghetto, fighting the Nazis. We had this news because sometimes the partisans would come into the ghetto to get money to help them with their fighting. When Reuven decided to join the partisans, a Jewish underground group, he wanted me to go, too. I told him, "No, you go ahead. If everything works out, I will come see you. I will go, too." When Reuven left the ghetto that day, it was the last time I ever saw him.

I later found out that while he was in the partisans, he and his group were hiding. Two people from the Polish underground group, the A.K., went to where my brother's group was hidden. These men told my brother's group that they needed to go on a mission, but first, all their guns had to be checked over. The two men gathered up the hand grenades, all the handguns and machine guns, and then began firing at my brother's group. My brother was killed that day in February 1943. Three people from his group survived, as they had been left for dead.

These three survivors eventually made it back to Ostrowiec and told my cousin, Avram Soika, who was a contact person for the underground, what happened.

In the ghetto, what kept going through my mind was, "Where did my parents go? Where did my brothers and sisters go?" I didn't know at the time where they went. I later found out they had all been sent to Treblinka, the place of no return. The day after they had gathered in the big square, they were all marched down to the railroad station, and this is when Avram had seen them.

My cousin Avram worked outside the ghetto, as he worked for a high-ranking Nazi named Jäger, who was in charge of a distilling factory that made *spiritus* [100 percent alcohol made out of potatoes]. Avram lived in a room on the factory premises. His job was taking care of Jäger's horses, cows, and pigs. One day I was assigned to work in the spiritus factory to unload boxcars of potatoes, and I saw my cousin. Avram told me that once when he looked out of the window in his room and saw the many boxcars at the railroad station, he also saw people from the ghetto being loaded into the cars. Among those he saw being loaded into the boxcars were his wife and son, my family, and many of our relatives. The doors to the trains closed, and the train pulled out of the station. Destination unknown! He told me that he was told by the high-ranking Nazi, Jäger, that the transport that Cousin Avram had seen went to Treblinka, where the people would be murdered. On hearing this, I really broke down crying hard, as I knew I would never see my family again. My family was murdered in Treblinka. After the war, I learned that Treblinka was an extermination camp. The people went straight to the gas chambers and crematoria. Over a period of thirteen months, more than 800,000 innocent people were murdered by the Nazis in the Treblinka extermination camp because they were Jewish. Now I knew I would have to fight for my own survival—it was up to me to see that I would survive. That's all that went through my head, was survival. I never gave up my hope, belief, and positive thinking. Those three things kept me going.

Cousin Avram later escaped and spent the rest of the war years being hidden by a Polish woman.

The survivors of my brother's partisan group told Cousin Avram that the people responsible for killing my brother and the other members of his group were part of the Polish underground group *Armja Krajowa,* or A.K. [pronounced ah-kah]. This particular group was very, very anti-Semitic and said that Poland would be liberated by Poles only. My brother's group was made up of Jewish resistance fighters. When I finally talked to those three survivors, they told me they had seen Reuven shot and killed. They said they wished they had some of his poems to give me. This was little consolation, because now I was really alone. I was sixteen years old and all alone. Maybe the pain of the loss would have been easier if Reuven had been killed fighting the Nazis, but to have been killed by another partisan group just because he was Jewish was very difficult for me to understand.

12

Why Do I Have to Be a Part of This?

CLEANING UP THE OSTROWIEC GHETTO, LATE 1942–EARLY 1943. Polish people lived in the ghetto area but worked at their own jobs. All the Jews selected to stay in the ghetto were assigned some kind of job. People were assigned to work in the *Hermann Goeringwerke* factory melting steel, making steel plates, and building railroad cars. I remember seeing piles of utensils waiting to be taken to the open hearth used for melting the metal. Some people were assigned to look through the utensils, because some of the pots and pans had false bottoms where people had hidden their valuables. Those of us not working at the factory were assigned the task of cleaning out the belongings the Jews left behind in the big ghetto.

I was selected to help with cleaning out the big ghetto. They assigned me to work for an SS man, Sergeant Holtzer. My first task in going into a house was knocking on the walls with my hammer. If the walls were hollow, I had to rip away the wall covering and plywood, because it meant that the Jewish family who lived there must have hidden fur coats, silver, jewelry, or other valuables behind the walls. If they weren't hollow, I didn't bother ripping away the wall covering.

I always used to pray to God that the furniture inside the room was not too heavy. In those days, furniture was passed down from generation to generation and made of solid wood. The headboards on the beds were so heavy. I had to carry those pieces of furniture out one by one on my back with no help at all. As I carried the furniture out, I didn't dare show any signs of weakness on my face. Sergeant Holtzer watched me all the time to see if he could find any signs of weakness in me. If he did, this would be his excuse to shoot me. He could say I was weak and not doing my job properly.

Once the belongings were outside, we loaded them on a truck, and they went to a warehouse and were later sent to Germany. We went from house to house in this methodical way. Sometimes we would find a person hiding in a room, and they were immediately taken outside and shot. Sometimes we would find little children, and even babies, whose mothers left them behind, hoping a Polish family would find them and rear the babies as their own.

I remember one day going inside a home and seeing a beautiful doll on the floor. It looked as if it had been dropped because the mother couldn't grab her child and the doll, too. Sergeant Holtzer stepped inside the room, spotted it, and said, "Isn't that a pretty doll?"

"Yes, sir," I said.

I can still see the beautiful doll on the floor. This was no store-bought doll; Jews weren't allowed to leave the ghetto to buy things. This doll had been handmade by a mother for her child.

The mother made the doll using a piece of scrap material for the body and an embroidered sheet or pillowcase for a beautiful white dress. The mother drew a happy face on the doll so that when her child looked at the doll, a happy face would be looking back. When the child looked at its mother and father, it was always seeing sad faces.

Sergeant Holtzer looked at the doll again and said to me, "You better be careful with this doll. I'm going to take it home to my children. Be sure when you put this doll on the truck, put it in nice and neatly. Then when you unload the belongings and put them in the warehouse, be sure to keep it away from the pots, pans, and clothing."

I did as Sergeant Holtzer said; what choice did I have? My friends were also carrying out dolls some parents left behind, and we put them very nice and neatly in the warehouse.

A few days later, we came into a room, and Sergeant Holtzer said he didn't want to go in—it stank. I walked in and boy, did it smell! I heard a child crying and screaming—the parents had left it behind, hoping someone would save it. As I walked in, my whole body trembled. I asked myself, "Why me, a teenager? Why do I have to be a part of this?"

I walked over to the crib and picked up the small, screaming little child. Whenever I think about this child now, I always stretch out my arms. I can still feel the warmth. As I was holding the child, it was cuddling close to my body. It must have thought I was its mother. When I walked outside, I put the child on the pavement, but Sergeant Holtzer stopped me. Pointing, he said, "Take it to the tall building over there." My friends were also carrying small children to the top floor of this building.

As I walked out of that building, I was the happiest teenager! I was thinking that those children were going to be sent to Germany. Once in Germany, they would be adopted and reared as Germans, never knowing who their parents were. I was very happy, and I went on with my work cleaning out the rooms with a big smile on my face, thinking about their bright future.

A couple of hours later, I looked back at the tall building and saw an SS man open a window on the top floor. A group of five or six SS men were standing on the street below. The SS man standing at the window shouted to the SS men on the street, "Are you ready?" I can still see him.

They answered, "Yes!" They positioned their rifles toward the top window.

I said to myself, those dolls we stacked so neatly in the warehouse, they're not going to be taken home for their children to play with.

I can still see it today.

As I took a closer look, I realized the SS man was not holding a doll out of the window. He was throwing one of the small children we had carried upstairs out the window. He kept throwing the children down, one after the other, as the SS men took potshots at them. I can still see and hear those SS men smiling, laughing, and arguing about who had the best aim. To them, this was a lot of fun.

The sights I saw were horrible, but once again, I had to go on with my work. As we approached the next house, there was a small child left outside, wrapped up in a lot of blankets. I think the Polish family who was hiding a Jewish child was afraid of being caught. Hoping I could talk him out of harming the little child, I turned to Sergeant Holtzer and said, "Polish people are always leaving small children outside cuddled with lots of blankets to get used to the cold weather."

As the sergeant looked at the child, I said, "Sergeant Holtzer, you are not going to do it, are you?"

He told me if I said one more word I would get the same thing.

Honest to God, I didn't care. I said, "Sergeant, every day you come into work, you take out your picture of your seven children and wife at home. You always say, 'Aren't they beautiful? Wouldn't it be nice to go home, play with them, take them to the movies, and make love to my wife?'"

I kept talking. I took my life in my own hands. He took a sandwich from his pocket, took a bite, and put the rest back in his pocket. He took out his gun and put six shots into the little child. I can still hear the child screaming. I can see the little child looking at Sergeant Holtzer with bright eyes as if to say, "You couldn't kill me, could you?" He looked at the child, outraged and mad because he couldn't kill it. He grabbed the little feet with one hand and hit its head against the wall and silenced it.

During the day, the SS and the Gestapo were all the same. During the day, they killed little children, mothers, and fathers. At night, they went home with their bloody hands, played with their own children, and made love to their own wives. That's what one human could do to the other if we are silent and complacent. We must remember and never forget!

13

I Could Have Been Shot

STILL CLEANING UP THE OSTROWIEC GHETTO, EARLY SPRING 1943.
One day while working for Sergeant Holtzer cleaning out the ghetto, I walked into a room and heard something moving around upstairs. I took a bunch of utensils that had been left and threw them around, hoping the sergeant wouldn't hear. He did. "Go upstairs and see what is going on," he told me.

I went upstairs, came back down, and said, "Sergeant Holtzer, a bunch of rats are running around up there."

He said, "Why don't you go upstairs and count them?"

I came down and told him, "Sergeant Holtzer, I couldn't count them, because they were all running in different directions."

"Let's go upstairs," he said.

I told a lie, didn't I? I thought I could get away with it, but I could have been shot. When we got upstairs he said, "Rip away the floor." As the floorboards were loose, I easily lifted them up.

There was an old man hiding under the floorboards between the ground-level ceiling and the floor. I had to pull him out. He was so weak, he could hardly walk. God knows how many days he was without food and water. I put my arm around his body. He held a book in front of his face, and he was reading. He was tall;

I was short. I didn't know what he was reading. I spoke to him in all the languages I knew, but he didn't answer. As we walked down the steps, I could finally look into his book, and I realized he was praying Psalm 23, one of the traditional psalms said at Jewish funerals. "The Lord is my Shepherd, I shall not want. He makes me lie down in green pastures," and so forth. . . .

As we were walking in what had been the big ghetto, I said, "Sergeant Holtzer, let me take him to the small ghetto area. He has no food and no water. He is going to die anyway." The sergeant didn't answer. Suddenly, the old man stopped walking. I said to myself, I guess he is getting tired and cannot walk anymore.

All of a sudden, my face started getting wet. When I wiped my face it was not sweat, it was his blood. Sergeant Holtzer had shot him with the silencer. I let loose of the old man, and he fell to the pavement. After I dropped him, Sergeant Holtzer stepped in front of my face. He wanted to see what kind of expression I had, but I didn't give him the satisfaction. Anyone caught hiding in the basement, between the floors, in the ceiling, or in the attic, was taken out and shot in front of the house. I could have been shot, too.

I can still see Sergeant Holtzer today. He was a middle-sized man with a long face and light hair; maybe it was blond. He must have weighed about 170 pounds. One day I took a chance. I don't know, maybe I was just naïve, I took a chance. I really wanted to know what made him so cruel. I asked him, "Sergeant Holtzer, how can you kill small children without mercy when you have seven children of your own and a wife? You've shown me their picture."

He looked at me and said, "Do you see that fly on the wall? It is easier for me to kill a Jewish child than the fly on the wall."

He told me that when he killed the first child, he went home and could not sleep the whole night. When he killed the second child, he couldn't sleep half the night. After that, the third child and so on was just routine. I looked at him and went on with my work. We had other SS men who killed children, too, but Sergeant Holtzer was very mean.

There was a small street in Ostrowiec near the church. As I was walking in that area, I saw a woman arguing with an SS man.

"I am not Jewish!!" she said. Her name was Jetka Joab. I knew her. She was a good friend of our family and came from the same city, Konin. She was even born in Konin. She was arguing in Polish that she was not Jewish. She said, "As you can see from my papers, I'm not Jewish, I'm Polish." The SS man said, "Yes, you are Jewish." He took out his gun and shot her in the head.

As I was walking through the big square doing my job, an old woman came running up to Sergeant Holtzer, yelling in Polish. She was a small, skinny woman with an old dirty dress. She yelled in Polish that Jewish people were hiding. I can remember it like today. At first, the sergeant didn't pay any attention to her. Then, Sergeant Holtzer, who didn't speak any Polish, asked me, "What is she saying?" I said, "Sir, I don't understand. She is mumbling."

She didn't let up at all, again saying the same thing in Polish. Finally, she mustered the words, *"Jude, Jude, hutch, hutch, Jude, Jude."* [Jew, Jew, come, come, Jew, Jew]. The sergeant went with her while I waited. He came back with a family: a husband, wife, and a boy of nine or ten. My heart started to pound. I said to myself, Oh my God, I know those people, they are from my city, Konin. I went with their son Lutek to cheder and to public school. Their family name was Burzynski. Lutek was working in the steel mill that day.

Sergeant Holtzer approached me with the family and asked if I knew them. "I never met them in my life," I said. I looked at them, and I knew what was going to happen. The sergeant asked me, "Are they Jewish?"

"I am sure they are not," I told him.

Without any second thought or remorse, he took out his gun and shot the wife. He waited for the expressions on the faces of the little boy and the husband. He then shot the little boy, and the father.

I am sure the old woman was rewarded with ten kilos [twenty-two pounds] of sugar and a bottle of vodka for showing where Jewish people were hiding. It was a horrible scene, seeing the family of my friend I had known all my life killed. I never told him what happened to his family until after we were liberated.

– 14 –

I Could Make Somebody Very Rich

ORGANIZING IN THE SMALL OSTROWIEC GHETTO, 1943. We were enterprising even in the ghetto. Not only were there underground groups outside the ghetto, we had a group inside, as well. Being a good organizer, I soon became involved in the underground once my work with Sergeant Holtzer was finished.

I shared a room in the small ghetto with a man from Konin named Czerwonka. He was a very sick man with boils all over his face. I was afraid he would die. After Reuven left for the underground outside the ghetto, they added another man to my room, and I am sure he was not Jewish. His Polish was so perfect he did not have to stay in the ghetto. He could have lived anywhere, and nobody would have pointed the finger at him saying he was Jewish. I did not trust him at all, because he spoke good Polish and good Yiddish. This man started asking questions like where could he buy some guns and about other underground activities. At this point, I really became suspicious and never answered his questions. I thought he was a spy put in the room to learn about what was going on in the ghetto.

One day, the commandant of the underground group came to me and said, "Mendel, we need to get weapons. The German troops are coming our way, and we must defend ourselves." It just so happened that one time when I was outside the ghetto, I made an acquaintance with a German sergeant. This sergeant hated Hitler and said, "We would be winning the war if Hitler was not busy fighting Jews." Because he hated Hitler and the SS, I decided to take a big chance and asked him if he had any guns he wanted to sell.

I said, "If I could buy some guns, I could make somebody very rich."

He looked at me in such a way that he must have thought I was crazy, and asked, "Are you kidding?"

I looked back into his eyes and said, "No, I am not kidding. How much do you want for a gun?"

"Twelve hundred marks," he said.

I met with the underground commandant and told him about the guns and how much they would cost. He looked at me in disbelief. "We don't have that kind of money," he said. "However, there are some very rich people who brought lots of money with them into this ghetto. They still have it, we need to have guns, so we need to get the money." He got the money, and I arranged to meet the sergeant outside the small ghetto. I would go through the wooden fence to the other side and cross the street to our meeting place.

I was not worried about getting caught, because I had some Polish identification papers. Inside the ghetto was a young man of about nineteen. He was a very good forger. He could sign the mayor's signature so well that the mayor himself wouldn't know this was not his own writing. I felt very protected because of my Polish papers and my blond hair.

I would take the money to the German sergeant and pay him 1,200 marks for each gun. I brought the guns back inside the ghetto and gave them to Avraham, the leader of the underground. One day Avraham came to me and said, "Mendel, we took one of the guns you got into the forest to shoot it, but it didn't work. When we started to cock it, it wouldn't work."

"Do you have the gun?" I asked him.

"Yes," he said.

"Well then, give it to me, and I'll get another one."

I took the gun, put it inside the waistband of my pants, and covered it with my jacket. I left to go toward the *Kaserin* [soldiers' quarters], because I had not seen the sergeant in a while, and I knew this was where he was staying with the other soldiers. I walked up to the little guardhouse outside the main gate. As I walked up, the soldier standing guard looked at me and said, "Hey, where are you going?" I was dressed like a very poor little Polish boy.

I looked him in the eye and said, "I am going to work in the kitchen over here."

The guard let me pass because he knew the soldiers inside did not want to clean and would be very happy to have someone else do the dirty work. I walked in, went straight to the kitchen, took a broom, and started sweeping the kitchen floor.

Soon the sergeant came in for lunch. When I saw him I said, "I want to see you."

He told me, "Let's go to the latrine." Once we were inside the latrine the sergeant asked, "What are you doing over here? Why do you want to talk to me?"

"You sold me a gun, and it doesn't work. Here it is; it's broken. I want a new gun to replace the defective old one."

At this point, I was in a great deal of danger. All he had to do was to give a signal. "I could report you," he said.

"Yes, sir," I said, "But you will also get shot, because I have everything figured out." I pointed to my pocket as I said, "I have all the serial numbers in my pocket for all the guns that you sold me. Now I want a new gun to replace this one. I paid lots of money for it, and the money is not easy to find."

The sergeant looked around and thought for a minute, because what I said was true about his getting shot, too, if anybody found out about the guns. Finally he said, "Okay. You wait over here. I'm going to go up to my room and get another gun."

Just as he started toward the door, I stepped right in front of him. "Oh, no, you are not going to get the gun by yourself. We are going to go together."

Although he sold guns to me for the underground, I never trusted this sergeant. He could have turned me in without blinking an eye. Because we were walking together to his room, nobody bothered me. All the other soldiers were saluting him and just assumed I must be doing a job for him. Once we got to his room, he went to a box and handed me another gun. "Okay, now you can go," he said, motioning for me to leave.

Again, all he would have to do is turn me in, so I said, "No, we are going to walk out together. You are going to help me get past the sentry and then a block farther out. I don't want anything to go wrong."

He knew he did not have a choice, so he walked me through the gate and to the corner of the street and said, "Okay, now you go!"

I took off as fast as I dared without causing anybody to question what I was doing or where I was going. As quickly as I could, I went back to the leader of the underground and handed him the new gun. When I told him what I had done, he looked at me as if he wanted to kill me. "You are crazy!" he shouted. "You could have been killed. Then we wouldn't have our contact anymore."

Looking him in the eye, I said, "I took a chance. You remember I always take a chance, and I didn't want to be cheated. I took a chance, and everything worked out okay." I never saw the sergeant again after that, but we continued our underground work trying to obtain more guns outside the ghetto.

The next day, before I could leave the ghetto to do more organizing, the ghetto was surrounded by the German SS and the Polish police. They announced over the loudspeakers that no one was allowed to leave the ghetto. This was to be our last day. With the ghetto surrounded like that, there was really nothing the people inside could do. I figured the SS men would come in and take everyone out to the cemetery, where we would be shot.

I decided not to remain inside the ghetto. I was going to take a big chance and try to escape. I knew that if I got caught, the SS men would shoot me on the spot. I thought that if I could get away and join a partisan group to work in the underground, I might have a chance. I walked over to the ghetto wall and knocked out two wooden planks to make a hole big enough to fit my body through. I put some towels under my arm and got ready to leave.

Just then, a woman came over and asked me if I was going to run away from the ghetto. I asked her if she was going to run away. She said, "Yes."

I said, "Okay, go ahead, you go first."

She did not move. I looked at her; it was as if she was thinking. Then she said, "No, you go first."

I did not hesitate for an instant. With the towels under my arm and my false identification papers in my pocket, I left the ghetto.

I wanted her to go first, because if the SS were stationed outside the wall, she would have been shot, and I would have known not to go out. She also knew that if she went out first she might get shot. I'm sure she was thinking the same thing I was.

15

I Looked Like a Little Polish Kid

ESCAPING THE SMALL OSTROWIEC GHETTO, 1943. By the time I escaped from the ghetto, it was already after 9:00 P.M. The curfew had long since passed for Jewish people in the ghetto, and at 9:00, all the non-Jewish people had to be off the streets. I walked along whistling, just a happy-go-lucky little boy. I saw an SS man looking at the identification card of someone else. I quickly looked to see if there was another way to go, but there was not. I couldn't go back inside the ghetto without getting caught. The only thing for me to do was to go forward like nothing was happening. I was singing a little Polish song, just a happy-go-lucky guy. I walked by the SS man, who looked over at me and said, "*Guten Abend*," [good evening] and then went back to interrogating the other man. He didn't pay any attention to me. After I passed him, I was still trying to decide which way to go in order to get out of the city without getting caught.

In front of me was a hill. If I walked there, I would have to pass Gestapo headquarters. This was not any good at all. To my left were fields and orchards. I figured if I went that way, the dogs would start barking, causing people in the neighborhood to signal the SS. The people would start screaming, and the SS would pay attention and investigate. The guard was still interrogating the man, so the best way for me was to go to my right, toward the Jewish cemetery, which also shared a wall with the ghetto.

I was walking as fast as I could in order to get out of the city. I figured I needed to go straight to reach a small street I knew about. I thought if I could get to the street, I wouldn't have to worry. Once I got two or three hundred yards, away from the ghetto, there were fields of corn and wheat I could use as a cover.

I was walking along, minding my own business, when I heard someone yelling, "*Stehen bleiben!*" [Stop!] I kept walking— after all, I'm just a Polish guy and I don't understand German. This person kept screaming, "*Stehen bleiben!*" and I kept walking until I heard "*Stoje!*" [Stop!]. Now he was yelling for me to stop in Polish. At this point, there was nothing more I could do, so I stopped and froze where I was standing. The SS officer called to me from across the street and motioned for me to come over. I did not have a choice, so I crossed to the other side of the street.

I could not believe my eyes. The SS man was Sergeant Holtzer! Inside my belt I had a little gun, a Belgian lugar. I realized I had only one choice if something happened. "*Ausweis!*" [Papers] he said. He wanted to see my identification card. He took one look at the name on the card, "Marjan Jakubowski," then asked me where I lived. I told him I was living in an apartment close to the steel mill.

"It's late—after curfew—after 9:00," he said. Where do you work?" he asked.

Quickly, I answered, "I am working at the Hermann Goeringwerke factory making steel."

"What is your occupation?" he asked sharply.

"I am a bricklayer to build the ovens," I answered.

The sergeant was still looking at my identification card when he asked, "Do you know you are walking after curfew?"

"No, sir, I am not," I answered.

He looked at me sharply. "What do you mean you are not?"

I said, "On my watch I have ten minutes before nine."

"Where are you going?" he asked.

"I am going to my aunt's house," I told him. "She sent word to me that her stove is broken and she needs me to replace some bricks on it in order to fix it."

Sergeant Holtzer looked at me again. I was amazed that he did not recognize me from when I used to work for him. Maybe it was because my clothes were torn and I looked like a little Polish kid. I remember him making a comment about my hair and how it looked like *Der Führer's* hair because of the way it was always falling in my face.

While Sergeant Holtzer was talking, my mind moved like lightning. I knew that as long as he didn't recognize me, I would be fine. I kept watching his hands. He had a big cuff on the sleeve of his coat, and as long as he didn't put my identification papers into his coat cuff, I was okay. I knew if he made a move to put my card in his coat cuff, he would arrest me and have me shot. I would have no choice but to shoot him with the little gun I had with me and run. He looked at my identification papers one more time. Then his voice took on a different tone, "You better get, quick!"

Once he told me to go, I didn't stop to ask any questions. I took off. I know that if anybody had seen the back of my feet, there must have been sparks coming up from my heels, I was going so fast. Finally, I came to a field and stopped to take a deep breath. When I started walking again in the field, I saw a silhouette coming toward me. I hid behind the wheat. As the shadow came closer to my hiding place, I recognized the person as Urbach, who was also from Konin.

When I recognized Urbach, I came out from behind the wheat. "What are you doing over here?" I asked him.

"I am going back to the ghetto to get some money," he said. He didn't know the ghetto had been surrounded and if he went back, the SS would shoot him.

"Urbach," I said, "You cannot go back to the ghetto tonight. The Germans have it surrounded, and if you go back, you will be shot."

"But I have to go back!" he said urgently. "If I don't get the money, the people hiding us will kick us out!"

When the Nazis first surrounded the ghetto, some of the Jewish people arranged to go into hiding with Polish families outside the ghetto. The Jewish people had to pay so much money to the Polish to be hidden.

I undestood that he needed the money, but he had to stay alive too. "Urbach," I insisted, "I am sure you have some money hidden, but if you go another 200 yards toward the ghetto, you will get shot. Don't go to the ghetto."

He didn't listen and started walking toward the ghetto.

I stepped in front of him and said, "Urbach, if you go one more step forward, I will kill you! You will get shot anyway, and it is better that you die at the hands of a person who knows you than to go over there and get killed by the Germans. I will tell you one more time. Don't go!"

We stood there face to face for a few minutes while Urbach thought about it and finally decided not to go for the hidden money. He didn't say another word, just turned around on the path and went back in the direction he had come from. I saw this as an opportunity to go into hiding, so I started walking with him. After a few minutes, Urbach turned to me and said, "Where are you going?"

"I am going with you, Urbach," I said. "You have a hiding place, and I need a place to stay."

We walked together a while longer, and he began begging me not to go with him. "Look, Mendel. We do not have much room where we are, and we do not have enough money to pay for you, and there is not enough food."

I was not going to be pushed aside. "Urbach," I said, "You do not have any choice. I am going with you."

We continued walking together. Neither of us could go to the home of the Polish family until late at night, otherwise the neighbors would know what was going on. We walked the whole evening with Urbach begging me not to come with him. There was not enough room or money for an extra person and definitely not enough food. Finally, I decided there was no way I could go with Urbach to hide. He would not be talked into such a thing.

"Let's compromise," I said. "Why don't you give me some money to buy a bottle of vodka so I can get drunk." I didn't really need the money, but this was a graceful way to leave. Urbach reached into his pocket, took out a zloty, and handed it to me. Without another word, he left. I took the zloty and went in the direction of a little store that sold dry goods, vodka, other spirits, and groceries.

I knew the woman who owned the store from all the trading I had done when my brothers were tailors. I would go around the area to the stores and farms, selling the suits, coats, and pants they made and trading for food. I often traded in the store with her. Luckily, her husband was not there, as he was a very anti-Semitic person who would have called the Gestapo in a minute. She was very nice. She asked me what happened, and I told her about my family. I also told her about the ghetto being surrounded and deciding to run away.

As we talked inside the store, we could hear the SS trucks, cars, and motorcycles driving up and down. When they stopped in front of the store, I looked at the lady and said, "Give me vodka. My name is Marjan Jakubowski, and I am working for you in the fields. That's all you have to say. Give me a bottle of vodka!"

I put some vodka in my mouth and hair so I would smell like vodka and put my head down on the counter, pretending to be drunk. I heard the Germans come in the store. They said to her, "Some people have run away from the ghetto. Have you seen anyone?"

She shook her head no.

The officers walked over to me; I could feel them standing beside me. "Who is he?" they asked.

"Marjan Jakubowski," she answered.

"What is he doing over here?" the officer demanded.

She walked over in a very disgusted manner and said, "He works for me on the farm in the fields. He's dead drunk now. He's always coming in here after he finishes a job, and he gets a few pennies. He's always getting drunk."

While they were talking, I still had my head on the counter. One of the officers grabbed my head by the hair to get a better look at my face. Suddenly, he just let my head go. "BOOM!!" I had to let my head drop because I was playing like I was drunk. It hurt so much I thought I was going to break the countertop with my head. After that, I could hear the German saying, "He's so dead drunk, you can raise his head and let it fall, and he doesn't even know." I stayed in that position until I heard the Germans drive away.

As soon as the Germans left, I was not drunk anymore. I was alert and ready for the next step. Suddenly, the woman came to me and said, "You have to go right now before my husband comes back." I knew she was right. Although I wanted to stay longer, I knew it was not safe for either one of us. I took a bottle of vodka and quickly left the store.

16

They Looked at Me Like
I Was a Ghost

LIFE OUTSIDE THE SMALL OSTROWIEC GHETTO, 1943. When I left the general food and clothing store, I ran as fast as I could to a barn on a neighboring farm. I knew about the barn from my travels outside the ghetto, selling clothes my brothers had made. Inside the barn was a tremendous amount of straw and hay for the animals. It was perfect for me. I dug a very deep hole and pulled the hay over me so that it looked normal. I made sure I was near the wall that had cracks in it so I would be able to see outside and have some fresh air. All night long, I could hear the Germans and their cars going up and down the main road. They were talking in High German voices, looking for runaways from the ghetto. They must have found the hole in the ghetto wall where I escaped.

The Germans stopped the farmer, who was in front of his house, and asked him, "Have you seen any Jewish people?" The farmer must have said no, since he did not know I was in his barn. I guess they were not satisfied, though, because they later came into the barn, took pitchforks, and poked around in the hay. I was buried so deep they could not reach me. When the Germans were satisfied that no one was hiding in the barn, they left the farm. I stayed deep inside that hay until the next morning, when I dug myself out.

I walked outside the barn, and the farmer looked at me. "What are you doing here?" he yelled at me.

"What do you mean, what am I doing?" I asked him.

"The SS men were here," the farmer said. "You know we would have all been killed if they found you?"

"I know they were here. I was buried very deep in the hay, so you didn't have anything to worry about," I told him.

He looked at me again and said, "I want you to leave now. You can't stay here." He handed me some bread and salami, and I went on my way.

Walking away from that farm outside Ostrowiec, I decided to go to the house of the forest ranger. He lived in a duplex at the edge of the forest. I knew him and he was a good friend, so I asked him if I could stay, and he said yes. His neighbor, who lived in the second part of the duplex, was also a forest ranger, but didn't get along with him. The two rangers never spoke to each other. We both knew he was taking a tremendous risk, hiding a Jewish person, but he told me I could stay, although I would make the fourth person in his home. I lived with the ranger for about two months. His rooms were small, and each of the sleeping areas was partitioned by white sheets. I slept close to the wall. I was eating with his family, sleeping with them, and I liked the forest ranger's sister-in-law. I was even going into the village to the Catholic church with them. They were surprised and impressed that I knew the prayers by heart. What they didn't know was that I had gone to school with Catholics and learned the prayers. The people in church always asked the ranger who I was and what I was doing there. I told the ranger to tell them I was sent from Krakow to tell them which trees to cut down and send back to Germany, and so that's what he told people.

From time to time, SS officers would come to the forest ranger's house, always asking the same question: Had the ranger seen any partisans? The ranger always told them no, he had not seen any partisans. One day, the SS men asked the ranger who I was. The ranger told the SS men the same story he told people at church. I was laughing and having a good time staying there with the ranger and his family.

One day, the other ranger who lived next door looked at me and said, "What are you doing over here?"

"I have been sent from Krakow to inspect the trees that are to be cut down to be sent back to Krakow, then to Germany. Didn't you get the letter?" I asked.

He shook his head, "No, I didn't get any letter."

He stayed a little longer, asking more questions.

After he left, the ranger I was staying with became very concerned. He came to me and said, "Marjan, you must leave. It is not safe for you here anymore. I have a brother who lives near Opatow, and he is a farmer. He will be able to register you as a farmer, and then you can go to Germany as a farmer."

I thought the idea was tremendous! If I could get away from Poland to Germany as a farmer, nobody would know who I was. I had Polish papers, and everything would be just fine. It didn't take me long to get ready to leave. Before I left, I took the pictures of my family I had managed to save from the ghetto and hid them in the ranger's barn between the straw of the roof. I hoped that way they would stay dry. I told the ranger, "Someday I will return. I hope you can save these pictures for me."

That ranger was an example of a person we called a "Righteous Gentile." A Righteous Gentile was someone, man or woman, who was willing to hide Jewish people. These Gentiles hid Jews even though they endangered themselves and their families. If the Gentiles were caught hiding Jews, both families were shot. The ranger's sister, who was also my age and lived with him, walked with me to the edge of the forest, crying and embracing me and telling me good-bye.

After I left the ranger's house, I walked in the direction of the fish hatcheries. I could see a group of people walking toward me. As they came closer, I decided to get off the road. I could see they had a man watching them, and I didn't know if he was an SS man or Gestapo. The people in the group looked very familiar to me. As the group passed by me on the road, I turned to look at them one more time. Suddenly, I recognized a guy I used to work for. He was a Polish engineer, and the SS were using him to build fish hatcheries outside Ostrowiec. With him were a bunch of Jewish men and boys passing by me, going to work. I couldn't believe it—there were still Jewish people in Ostrowiec. They had not all been killed like I thought!

When the SS liquidated the small ghetto the night I escaped, everyone from the ghetto was placed in a camp outside the steel mill, surrounded by barbed wire. Some of the people worked in the steel mill, others in the brick factory, and some were finishing building the fish hatcheries. Before he was taken to Treblinka, my brother Szlama worked building the fish hatcheries.

"Hey!" I called out, but they just kept walking. I called their names. "Hey, guys! What's the matter with you, are you scared of me?" Still they didn't answer, as if they were afraid. There was no guard, only the engineer responsible for them.

All of a sudden, one of the guys said, "Take a look who's over here! It's Mendel!" They looked at me like I was a ghost.

"Hey, what's the matter with you guys?" I asked.

They looked at me again and said, "You were shot. They killed you as you tried to escape the ghetto, and we buried you."

I felt my body with both hands. "I don't think so," I said. "I'm still alive. Why did you think I was shot?"

Apparently, the night the Germans surrounded the ghetto, my roommate, the man I was suspicious of, decided to just walk out the front gates. The Gestapo shot him because they thought he was trying to escape. When the guys in the ghetto buried him, they thought they were burying me. It was dark, and this man also had blond hair.

They told me this story as we walked. In a split second I asked them, "Where are you staying?"

The group leader said, "They have built a camp in Ostrowiec, and we are staying there."

"How is it?" I asked, thinking of going back with them.

They stopped and thought for a minute and said, "It's okay. We go out to work in the brick factories, the steel mill, and other places. Then we come back—it's not so bad. The Ukrainians are watching over us, and we have some pretty good food because we can still organize things. The guards don't bother us too much."

After hearing what they had to say, I thought about staying on the outside with the Polish people, and I decided I would be better off going back to camp. I knew I could always walk away.

Getting back into camp was pretty easy. The Ukrainians were not counting people very closely. Everybody was counted going out to work and again coming back from work, but I easily slipped back into camp. Once inside, I was assigned to work in the brick factory.

17

I'm Sure Fortunes Were Melted This Way

LIFE INSIDE THE OSTROWIEC WORK CAMP, 1943. The conditions inside the work camp were not too bad, if you ignored the fact that it was very crowded and there were lots of lice. It was a small camp just inside the city. Barbed wire and lookout towers surrounded the camp. There were two barracks for the men and one for the women. The women's barracks had windows. The kitchen was on the women's side.

We slept in wooden bunks stacked two levels high, with two or three people sleeping in each bunk. We slept on straw mats that were on each of the bunks, and there was one blanket for each bunk. The straw mats had big bugs in them, and if they bit you, you jumped from the sting. The camps were very unclean.

There was a pond across from the camp by the factories. We walked on muddy roads going to work, and when it rained we would be up to our ankles in mud. We had lots of mosquitoes after a rain. The mosquitoes were so large that they could carry you away. We all had many mosquito bites. At night, when you turned your shirt inside out, it was full of lice. We used to kill them. Some of the prisoners [captives] used to pick them and eat them; I could never do that. I could not stand it. I could not understand why they did this.

One of the guys told me it was their own blood. They figured it was good blood. They said, if they're going to eat my blood, I'm going to eat theirs. People were hungry. People were dying of hunger.

Some of the men and women worked in the kitchen. Most of the men worked in the steel mill or the brick factory. I worked in the brick factory; it was very hot, very difficult again.

We were working hard, ten or twelve hours a day. It made no difference in winter. It was very cold, ten degrees below zero. We wore civilian clothes in that camp. We had a shirt, pants, and a jacket, but I was still cold. I found some paper cement bags and put them under my shirt to keep me warm. I used to say to myself, as long as I don't get sick from typhus, I will survive.

The food was not like the food we had at home. Before we went to work in the mornings, they gave us a slice of bread and synthetic coffee. At lunchtime, we had a type of soup. The soup always looked funny; there was a reddish color to it. Finally, we figured out this was because they were using horse meat to make the soup. It was disturbing, but at least we had meat. Overall, things were not so bad at this time. Besides the food we got, we still organized food from some of the Polish people. I remember we used to organize grits and cook them on a small stove in the barracks. It was so nice, because a little bit made a lot of food. I sprinkled a lot of sugar on those grits; they were so good. Even today, whenever I go to a restaurant, I will order grits with breakfast.

One day, when I was working with a group of men, we were put to work breaking rocks. We were in a line and breaking the rocks into small pieces to be used for a highway. An SS man walked up and down behind us as we worked. Suddenly, the man on my left fell over—he had been shot by the SS man. I kept working, although my hands were bleeding because of the sharp rocks. The man on my right fell over—he had also been shot by the SS man. This is another time when I believe Someone upstairs looked out for me that I should survive and tell the story.

Although things weren't so bad, we were always being watched, not by the Germans, but by the Ukrainians, to make sure we couldn't run away. There were no crematoria in Ostrowiec, and people were not usually randomly killed, but they worked us to death. For a short time, I worked at the steel mill, where my job was to check out the pots and pans brought from different cities that the Jews had left behind. We had to see if there were any double bottoms. First we had to hit the bottom of the pan against the table and listen to the sound. If there were a double bottom, it would sound hollow. We had to rip the bottom open with a small hatchet. Sometimes there were rings, jewels, or money hidden in the pans; other times the pots and pans were empty.

We also had to separate the aluminum pots from the copper pots and steel ones, so that they could all be melted down again and the metals reused for other things. We were supposed to put all the valuables, including money, into a pile, but sometimes those items made it into our pockets. I also took items from the pile of valuables so I could exchange the money or jewels for food from the Polish workers. Sometimes we didn't look so carefully inside before we put the pots and pans in the pile to be melted. I'm sure there were fortunes melted down this way.

After a few days working in that steel mill, I heard that somebody working in the brick factory died. I asked if I could take his place, so I was reassigned to the brick factory. Every morning, the Ukrainians marched us to the brick factory and we didn't see them again until the end of the day when they marched us back to camp. The railroad ran right into the brick factory. Even though I made bricks, I also had to go down to the railroad and help unload the open gondolas carrying special sand we used for brick making. The guards always told us that if we unloaded the gondolas very fast, we could rest. I had a good partner, and we were very quick. We unloaded the car in maybe two or three hours. When we were finished, we rested.

One day, a person from the underground approached me. "Mendel," he said, "We want you to derail a train."

I looked at him and said, "You are crazy! I cannot derail a train!"

He looked at me again and said, "I want you to derail a train. The people in the underground, the resistance fighters, said you could do it."

I took his word, since I had no reason to believe he wasn't really a member of the underground.

When I walked away from work that day, I said to my sand-unloading partner, "When they ask you where I am, tell them I finished unloading the gondola, and I am resting somewhere." As I said this, I pointed in the other direction and walked away. I found a small wrench among the tools and put it in my pocket. Then I walked to a nearby village and went into a farmhouse. I told the farmer, "I want a cow."

The farmer looked at me like I was crazy and said, "I cannot give you a cow. If the SS come to count and find one missing, my whole family will get taken out and shot."

After the Germans occupied Poland, all the farmers had to report how many cows, chickens, geese, pigs, and horses they had. The Germans would come around and double-check. If the counts were wrong, the whole family would be shot. Thinking about this, the farmer told me, "No, I cannot give you a cow."

I looked back at him. "Oh, yes, you can. Here is a note from the partisans saying they were here, and they wanted a cow. The partisans took it, and you had no choice because they had guns. The Germans will believe you. I want the longest rope you have and the cow. Now, when I walk away from here, if you run to the SS, your family will get shot anyway, because the partisans are close to your farm. They know I am over here to get the cow. Don't you dare tell."

He finally realized he had no choice, so he agreed. "No, we won't tell," he said.

I took the cow to the railroad tracks, where she started to graze. In Poland, the railroad belongs to the government, and grass grows on both sides of the track. When a poor person had a cow, sheep, or goat but no farm or place to feed it, they used the railroad right-of-way for grazing.

Once I reached the railroad, I saw German police walking along the tracks, checking the rails. I heard them talking about an important train coming through. This was a *Panzer* train, which had very thick steel-plated walls on the sides of each gondola car with cannons inside the walls facing the outside. These gondola-car walls were so thick that a bullet could not penetrate them. The cannons could be fired as the train passed through towns and cities. When the German police saw me, they tried to tell me to get away. I don't know how I did it, but I pretended to be deaf and mute. I looked like a poor peasant boy because my pants had holes in them and my shirt was torn. They talked to me in German, but I did not respond. I heard them saying, "He's a *Dummkopf*. He doesn't understand what we are talking about."

Finally, the German police were through checking the rails and started thinning out. After they left, I went to the track and put my ear close to it. I could hear the track vibrating, so I knew the train was coming. I took out the little wrench I brought with me and loosened the bolts on the plates holding the tracks together. When I finished, I put some dirt and grass over everything so no one could see what I had done.

I put my ear to the rail again. The vibrations were louder this time, so I knew the train was very close. I had only a little bit of time to get out of the way. I left the cow by the tracks and ran up a nearby hill. I waited on the hill until the train came. When it hit the unbolted part of the tracks, the train derailed with a tremendous explosion. I never saw what happened to that cow—I guess she was barbecued.

After the explosion, I went down to the village and told the people to leave everything and go to the forest. I knew the Nazis were going to come and kill everyone in retaliation for the explosion. Then I went back to the brick factory just like nothing had happened. My friends asked me, "Mendel, where have you been?"

"Oh, I was just out trying to organize something," I said, and went on with my work. The underground didn't try to contact me again while I was in Ostrowiec. I think the partisans in that area must have moved further into the forest.

Day in and day out, we went to work in the brick factory, which was about two to three kilometers away, and then returned to camp. Some people tried to escape by going under the barbed wire. If they could make it under the wire, they only had to crawl two or three hundred feet to escape. Some of them made it; some were shot. I thought about escaping, but felt I was more secure in camp.

Inside the camp, we were sometimes able to get a newspaper. We could hear the soldiers and SS men talking about how proud they were that the German army was going so deep into Russia. By 1944 the Russians were coming closer to Ostrowiec. One Russian tank even came into the city, but it drove away. I had one friend who was quick and jumped on the side of the tank as it left. As far as I know, he escaped. I would have run away, too, but at the time I was working above the ovens in the brick factory, and it was very hot. I was only wearing underwear. When I saw the tank from the window, I tried to quickly get dressed, but it drove away, and I was too late. The tank had disappeared.

– 18 –

Now You Are
a Number

AUSCHWITZ-BIRKENAU, 1944. After the Russians left, I figured the SS were going to bring everyone back to the camp, so I went to a man named Newman. Newman was a tremendous cabinetmaker; he had golden hands. He had a room in the same house as the German in charge of the factory, where his family lived. The house was located on the factory premises. Newman made furniture, beautiful hand-carved boxes, and other items for this German civilian. I went to Newman and asked him about going into hiding together. We went upstairs into the attic where the German family lived and hid for about three days. I don't know what happened, maybe someone told the Germans we were up there, or maybe they heard us moving around.

Suddenly, we heard a gruff voice—*"Kommen Sie herunter!"* [Come down!] At first we did not go down, but when they yelled louder, we realized they knew we were there, and we had no choice but to leave the attic. Going down the stairs, I said to Newman, "Why don't we say Psalm 23?" I figured we were going to get shot as soon as we got down, and this would be our final prayer. We knew that whenever the Germans caught someone hiding he or she was taken out and shot. This time, the Germans didn't shoot us. I heard them saying, "Let's save the bullets. Where they are going, they'll be killed anyway." I didn't know what this meant, but it did not sound good. We were very lucky they didn't shoot us right there.

It was early in the summer of 1944 when the Nazis put us back in the work camp, where we waited a few days. The Nazis came and marched us to the railroad siding, which was about fifty yards away, and ran along the side of the camp. They put us into boxcars attached to freight cars and an engine. We traveled quite a few days to an unknown destination. We knew we were attached to other freight cars, because we could see them when we went around a curve. Sometimes, when the train stopped, we were given soup, but this was very seldom. Some of us could look out the windows and see what cities we were passing through. They called out, "Katowice," "Sosnowiec," "Krakow," and "Oswiecim" [Auschwitz]. The boxcars were pushed into a camp called Birkenau, Auschwitz II. At the time, I did not know what camp we were in.

I was later told that there were actually three camps at Auschwitz. Auschwitz I was the main camp. Auschwitz II was Birkenau. Everybody that came into Auschwitz first had to go through Birkenau. We called Auschwitz III "Buna," as I. G. Farben had their rubber plant [Buna] there. I was told that this was where the Zyklon B cyanide gas, a nauseating, choking, poisonous gas, was made. When we reached the city of Oswiecim, they unhooked our cars from the freight cars and pushed us further into Birkenau. Birkenau was about two miles away from the main camp. When we reached Birkenau, the boxcar doors were opened. We stepped out to the sound of an orchestra playing classical music. I later learned that they picked the best musicians in Europe for that Birkenau camp orchestra. We saw SS men and prisoners who were going to clean the cars out walking up and down, smiling and laughing. I asked a prisoner, "What kind of camp is this?" His answer was a smile. I thought, "They are not allowed to tell us."

We could see the men's camp behind us, and across the ramp, also in Birkenau, the women's camp. I looked around and said to my friends, "My God, we came into a paradise here. Everything is so clean, and they have an orchestra playing for us.

Take a look at what kind of welcome we are getting over here." Across the ramp, behind a barbed wire fence, there were women smiling and waving at us. As I looked farther down to my right, I could see big chimneys with smoke coming out of them. I said to my friends, "This is a fine place. Look, they have big bakeries here. When they ask me what profession I am in, I will say I am a baker." I thought that if I could work in the bakery, I would always have enough food to eat, and I could organize more food for my friends.

As we waited on the ramp, the SS came and began selecting. The SS men were walking up and down. I stood up on my toes to look taller, looking them straight in the eyes. I was not sure what they were looking for, but because I was skinny and short, I wanted to be as straight and tall as possible. When the SS man pointed at people with his thumb up, the people went to the right; when he pointed with his thumb down, they went to the left. I was chosen to go to the right with some of my friends. Other friends were chosen to go to the left. I didn't know what right and left meant at the time.

During the selection process, I saw a man with a white coat walking around. I said, "Hey, guys, take a look! We came into a paradise! Bakeries over there, women welcoming us, the orchestra is playing, a doctor is walking up and down! If somebody faints or if somebody is sick, he is going to get help." I later found out he was Dr. Joseph Mengele, the Angel of Death, looking for twins for his experiments.

When the selections were over, the guards said, "Anyone chosen to the right will walk down toward those chimneys." I was in the first group to go to the right, and as we walked toward the chimneys, we began to smell something. As we came closer, my friends said, "You know, it doesn't smell like the aroma of bread. It smells like skin."

I smelled the air, too, and said, "You're right. It does smell like skin." I was always thinking positively, so I said, "You know what, they have so many people here, they must be killing lots of cows and horses for food. They cannot keep the animal skins lying around, so they are burning them."

We didn't know what they were baking, but we knew it was not the smell of bread. It was also not the smell of animals; it was completely different and very strong. I started to get scared. The hair on the back of my neck stood up, and my body started to shiver. My friends must have been scared, too, because they said, "Mendel, let's make a break and run away."

I looked around and saw the lookout towers and electrified barbed wire fencing. "There is no way to escape," I said.

As we came closer to the chimneys, we were taken into a big barrack and told to undress and leave everything behind. Completely naked, we waited for a little while. An SS man came in and shouted, "Everybody out!" We crossed the road to another building, which held the showers. Inside, we had to step into a little pool and stay there for a few seconds. Only God knows what kind of disinfectant was in that pool, because it was burning anyone who had boils or cuts on his feet. We stepped out of the little pool and went under showerheads, where we waited for the water to come. When the water finally came, it was so hot that if I could have held an egg under it, the egg would have been hard-boiled.

Everyone tried to move to keep from getting burned, but the SS guards were standing on the side with bullwhips. They were whipping anyone who tried to get out from under the hot water. After the hot water there came cold water, then the water was turned off. We left the showers. I saw a towel, which I quickly grabbed, dried myself, and went to another room along with the others, where we were given some clothes. These clothes weren't matched; some were too big and some too small. I got a shirt so big I could wrap myself in it five times. I traded shirts with another man standing near me, whose shirt was too small.

Some of the clothes were made of striped material; others were just civilian clothes. A yellow stripe was sewn on all of them so the guards could tell that we were Jewish. I saw other markings in the camp, as well. I later learned that each marking had a different meaning. Red stripes meant political prisoners; a purple triangle was for the Jehovah's Witnesses; and the Gypsies had a big black Z for *Zigeuner*. The homosexuals had a pink stripe, and the criminals, a green stripe.

Once we got our uniforms, we were taken to the quarantine camp. I heard later that the quarantine camp was not too far from the gas chambers and crematoria. As we walked inside the camp, we had to stretch out our arms to get a number. This number was tattooed very quickly on our arms, but they never deadened the skin. I watched my friends being tattooed. When it was my turn, I stretched out my arm, and they tattooed the number B4990. I held my fist very tight and never made a face at all. My arm was hurting, but I never made a face. I was not going to give them the satisfaction.

When it was over, the SS man looked at me and said, "Do you know what this number is all about?"

"No, sir," I answered.

"Now you are being dehumanized. You are not human anymore. You are a number, and you better remember this number, because that's what you will be called from now on."

They put the same number on my shirt on the yellow stripe, and so I became B4990. But in my mind, I was still a free person.

Konin city hall.

Konin, large city square.

Wooden bridge over the Warta River, which runs through Konin.

Konin Jewish cemetery, pre–World War II,
destroyed by the Nazis during their occupation.

Konin Public School that Mike Jacobs (Mendel Jakubowicz) attended from grades five through seven. Circa 1929.

Army officers' school in Konin, where Jews were detained from the time they were forced from their homes until they were deported to the Ostrowiec ghetto. Circa 1935.

Mike's brother
Avram.

Mike's sister
Ester.

Detail from photo, showing
Mike's brother Reuven.

Detail from photo, showing
Mike as a young boy.

Mike's brother
Szlama.

Cheder (*Hebrew School*) *students and some citizens gather to honor Philip Charof, a former resident of Konin who immigrated to the United States. He brought a donation of funds to the school when he visited Konin in 1935. The funds were from a "brotherhood" group in the U.S. who had all come from Konin. Charof is seated in the middle of the third row and is wearing a white hat. Mike is on the first row holding the right end of the banner.*

Mike's sister Ester with friend Avram Wiernik. Gniezno, Poland, 1929.

Mike's brother Avram (left) with friend. Konin, 1929.

Left to right: a friend, Mike's cousin's wife, Mike's cousin Hollander, Mike's sister Ester and her boyfriend Wolf Kaczka, Mike's brother Avram. Circa 1931.

Mike's cousins (clockwise from top left) Bluma, Gucia, Maricia, and Bronia Gerson, circa early to mid-1920s.

Mike's cousins who lived in Tuliszkow. Included are: Ester, Maricia, Bronia, Gucia, Bluma, and Regina Gerson. 1929.

92

Mike's brother Avram with friend Hanna, who later married his cousin Heniek Gerson. Konin, Poland, 1930.

Mike's cousin Yecheil Alter Jakubowicz, from Kleczew, who married Mike's cousin Regina Gerson, from Tuliszkow. Circa 1937.

Mike's brother Avram (left) with their cousin Avram Meir Szwam. Circa 1930.

93

Mike's brother Szlama on first row, far right, with friends. Circa 1935.

Mike's brother Avram (far left) with a group of friends. Konin.

*Mike's brothers Avram, back row, third from left, and Szlama, beside him,
with their cousins from Tuliszkow. Circa 1932.*

*Konin group of Young Pioneers, a Zionist Youth Group.
Mike's brother Reuven is on the far left of the last row.*

Michael "Mike" Jacobs (Mendel Jakubowicz) after his liberation from Gusen II, when he worked in the kitchen for the U.S. Army in Mittenwald, Germany. The U.S. Army issued him a uniform. 1945.

Above: Mike working for the U.S. Army. Mittenwald, Germany, 1946.

Mike and friends doing gymnastics. Mike is at the top of the pyramid. Mittenwald, Germany, 1946.

Mike baking matzohs *(unleavened bread) for* Pesach *(the Jewish holiday of Passover). Mittenwald, Germany, 1946.*

Mike (far right) marches with the Mittenwald Jewish soccer team to the stadium for their soccer game. Circa 1946.

*Survivors from Konin, Poland, gathered in Munich, Germany, in 1947.
Mike is third from the left in the front row.*

*Jewish soccer team of Mittenwald, Germany, which Mike organized and was captain
of. Mike is at the far right. Mittenwald. Circa 1946.*

Mittenwald soccer team at tournament of European countries. Included were soccer teams from Austria, Italy, Switzerland, and Mittenwald, Germany. The Mittenwald team won the tournament. Mike is the third man from the right, standing.

Mike (center) conducting a Hapoel Sports Organization business meeting. Mittenwald, Germany, 1947.

Mike (left) and boyhood friend Lutek (Leon) Burzynski. They survived all the war years together. Mittenwald, Germany, 1947.

Mike organized this soccer team in Breman, Germany, before leaving for the United States in July 1951. Mike is the fifth man from the left and captain of the team.

*Mike instructing a women's physical fitness group.
Mittenwald, Germany, circa 1946–1947.*

*Mike Jacobs (second from left) and his cousin Avram Soika with lady friends.
Mittenwald, Germany, circa 1947.*

Mike Jacobs wins the 400-meter (470 yard) race in competition in Bad Reichenhall, 1946. Mike also won the 100-meter (120 yard) race as part of the competition.

Mike wins the broad jump at 6.7 meters (21.91 feet) in the American-English Zone Survivors track meet in Landsberg and Bad Reichenhall, Germany, 1947–1948 competition. 1948.

Mike (far right) accepts his award of a loving cup from an official of the American-English Zone Survivors competition in Landsberg and Bad Reichenhall, Germany, 1948.

Mike with tournament officials of the American-English Zone Survivors Competition. 1948.

UNRRA citations for sports performance, organizing, leadership, development, and training.

UNRRA Team 568   MITTENWALD

A W A R D

TO
Mr. *Jakubowich Mendel*
of D.P. Camp Mittenwald is hereby granted
this Award for outstanding performance in
Light athletic ....
....
held .... *Landsberg* and Munich, German
in games sponsored by the YMCA.

HARRISON D. HOBSON
WELFARE OFFICER
OPERATION MITTENWALD   Mr. R. SPIER

SPORTS LEADER
OPERATION MITTENWALD   24.10.1946

Team 568   MITTENWALD

A W A R D

JEWISH SPORT CLUB
H A P O E L

FOR EXCELLENT PERFORMANCE AS A
SPORTS CLUB

FOR SUPERIOR ACHIEVEMENT IN
ORGANIZING SPORTS ACTIVITIES
AND

A PROVEN CHAMPION

HARRISON D. HOBSON
WELFARE OFFICER
OPERATION MITTENWALD   Mr. R. SPIER
DIRECTOR OPERATION MITTENWALD

A. YSRAEL
SPORTS LEADER
OPERATION MITTENWALD   24.10.1946

(Above)
Sports awards for soccer,
track and field.

Team 568   MITTENWALD

A W A R D

To the Leader of *Jewish Spl. Club Hapoel*
Mr. *Jakubowich Mendel*
for outstanding leadership in the development and training of the members of
the Sports Club .... *Hapoel* ....
Under your leadership this Club has not
only won 3 well deserved Championships
but has Contributed materially to the
physical develpment of a large proportion
of our Camp population.

HARRISON D. HOBSON
WELFARE OFFICER
OPERATION MITTENWALD   Mr. R. SPIER
DIRECTOR OPERATION MITTENWALD

SPORTS LEADER
OPERATION MITTENWALD   24.10.1946

This is to certify that

Mendel

was admitted to the United States on

at

as a Displaced Person immigrant for

under Sec. 5 of the Act of

and has been registered under the Alien Registration Act, 1940.

Visa Application No. I 176092

DATE OF BIRTH	SEX	HAIR	EYES	HEIGHT
Dec 29 1925	M	Blond	Green	5 0

Commissioner of Immigration and Naturalization.

GPO   16—48499-3

Permit for entrance to the United States.

Mike leaving on the train from Mittenwald to Breman, Germany, from where he will sail to the United States. July 1951.

105

Mike instructing gymnastics at the Jewish Community Center in South Dallas. 1952.

Mike speaking to a Southern Methodist University class. Circa 1971.

St. Mark's in soccer tournament, 1972. Mike, far right, referees.

Mike referees an international soccer game in Dallas.
Dallas Tornados vs. the Russian Moscow Dynamos, August 17, 1972.

Mike (third from right) explains Auschwitz-Birkenau to a Jewish Federation group of Greater Dallas. January 1978.

Mike explains what went on in Auschwitz-Birkenau in Poland to a group from the Jewish Federation of Greater Dallas while they stand in a Birkenau women's barrack. January 1978.

108

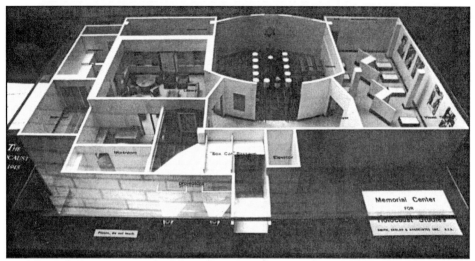

Original mock-up (model) of the Dallas Memorial Center for Holocaust Studies. 1983.

Mike, Ginger, and oldest son, Mark, being videotaped for Mike's interview with Ted Koppel on "Nightline." April 1983.

Mike connecting the cables holding the railroad boxcar to be unloaded onto the parking lot of the Dallas Jewish Community Center for the entrance to the Holocaust Center. September 15, 1983.

Mike checking the cables to make sure they are secure to lift the boxcar from the trailer to the parking lot.

Mike (far right) speaks at the dedication of the memorial room in the Dallas Memorial Center for Holocaust Studies, January 29, 1984. Survivor Martin Donald holds the Bronze urn containing human bone fragments Mike Jacobs brought back from the crematoria at Birkenau.Other Survivors are, right to left: Mike Shiff behind Martin Donald, Henry Goldberg, Ossie Blum, Frank Bell, Rosa Blum, and Jack Altman.

Inside view of the Memorial Room of the Holocaust Center.

Entrance to the Dallas Memorial Center for Holocaust Studies, showing the banisters that represent the railroad rails and steps representing the railroad crossties.

Front view of the Memorial Room of the Holocaust Center.

Walls with memorial stones for individuals in the Memorial Room.

View of the Memorial Room with the bronze sculpture, "Grasping for Life," the bronze Magen David casket, and six memorial lights. Twelve pillars with names of concentration camps are linked by a heavy wrought iron shaped barbed wire that surrounds the granite marble stone.

(Above) Display room with photographs and memorabilia of the Nazi era.

(Left) An actual boxcar used for transporting people to the concentration camps as an entrance to the foyer and museum rooms.

(Below) Display of cutlery and artifacts from concentration camps (these are from Auschwitz-Berkinau).

114

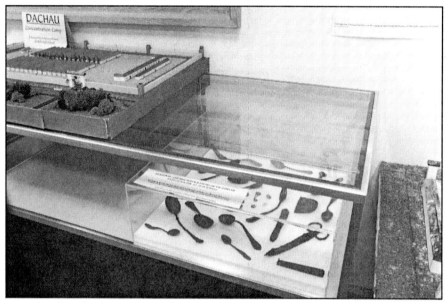

Display of cutlery, some artifacts with partial view of concentration camp model.

View of the foyer with pre-Holocaust photos and Judaica (like Phylacteries, talis or prayer shawl, and prayer books) items depicting pre-war Jewish life.

*Mike speaks to Whittier Middle School students in Norman, Oklahoma,
March 10, 2000.*

*Mike shows students at Whittier Middle School the Auschwitz tattoo on his left forearm
after speaking to them. March 10, 2000.*

Mike shows and explains his artifacts from concentration camps, which are: a pair of children's shoes, soap made of human fat, "Zyklon B" (cyanide), the hat he wore in Gusen II, and the "make-believe" watch he made in Gusen II, to students of Central Middle School in Putnam City, Oklahoma, May 8, 2000.

Mike autographs after speaking and explaining his artifacts to students at Duncan Middle School, Duncan, Oklahoma, April 13, 2000.

"Make-believe" watch Mike secretly fashioned when forced to labor as a machinist at Gusen II.

Prisoner hat Mike wore in Gusen II.

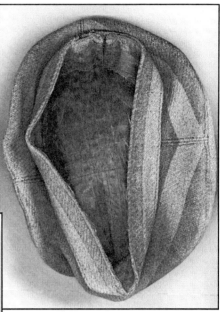

Bar of soap made with human fat.

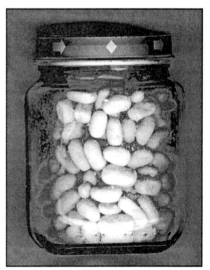

Zyklon B crystals used in concentration camp gas chambers.

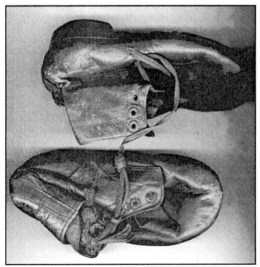

Child's shoes from concentration camp

(Above) Mike in women's barrack in Birkenau during Dallas Federation Mission, which he led. 1992.

Mike Jacobs
Thank You
For
Making A Difference
In The Lives Of
Hundreds Of Students
At
Garland High School

One hundred years
from now...
It will not matter
what my bank account was,
the sort of house I lived in,
or the kind of car that I drove.

But...
The world may be different
because I was important
in the life of a child.

HERSHEY'S
MILK CHOCOLATE
NET WT.
1.45 OZ. (41.5g)
'HERSHEL BAR'

PRESENTED TO
MIKE JACOBS
MAUTHAUSEN SURVIVOR
41st ANNIVERSARY
MAY 5, 1945 – MAY 5, 1986
GIVEN BY
HIS FRIENDS AND LIBERATORS OF
THE 11th ARMORED DIVISION

Restored synagogue in Konin, Poland, 1988.

Family photograph, 2001. Standing (l to r): Granddaughter Rivka Linksman, sons Andrew (Andy), Reuben, and Mark, son-in-law Wayne Linksman and daughter Deborah (Debbie). Seated, Mike and Ginger, and granddaughters Leeza, Aviva, and Sarah Linksman.

19

Everything in Camp Was Done to Music

INSIDE BIRKENAU, 1944. When the tattooing was finished, we were assigned to a barrack. We were in the quarantine camp a few days when an SS guard came in. He asked, "Who is a very agile person?" I raised my hand, because I was a good gymnast back in Konin. I thought that maybe they needed someone to climb posts or something. I kept looking for the other people from our transport, but I could never find them. Those chosen to go to the left had gone into a big building. I found out from the *Sonderkommando* later on that they went to the gas chambers. [The *Sonderkommando* were those prisoners whose job was to remove the corpses from the gas chambers.] The steel door was closed behind them, and they stood under the showerheads. They waited for water to come out of the showerheads, but no water ever came out. Instead, the SS put in Zyklon B. It took between twenty to thirty minutes for the people to suffocate to death. The men working in the Sonderkommando told me that if the SS men had put water in the gas chambers, it would have taken only between two to five minutes for the Zyklon B to dissolve and kill. I was also told that parents tried to cover the small children, hoping that they could breathe a little longer. People also tried to scratch holes in the gas chamber walls. The walls were so thick that they could not make the holes, but there were scratches on the walls. You can still see the scratches today.

After all the people were dead, the Sonderkommandos had to go inside with axes to separate them and remove the bodies. They found people piled one on top of the other, each trying to breathe a little bit longer. When the bodies were taken out, the Sonderkommandos had to remove any gold teeth. They shaved off all the women's hair. The bodies were taken to the crematoria to be burned. Other people later told me that the SS made lampshades from the human skin. From the hair, they made material, carpets, stuffed mattresses, and from the bones, fertilizer. Every part of the body was used. The prisoners who were Sonderkommandos told me that while people were burning in the crematoria there were buckets beneath to catch the human fat to make soap. The smell of the crematoria was very strong. Sometimes, when the wind blew in the wrong direction, it was very hard to breathe. There were so many transports filled with people coming into Auschwitz-Birkenau during 1944, the crematoria could not keep up with the number of people being killed. The Nazis started burning people in the pits.

One day I heard singing, and I said to myself, why did they sing in very young voices? I went to the back of my barrack. I opened the door and stuck a little of my head out. We were not supposed to open the door or walk out at night, and the searchlights went back and forth all the time. In the men's section, all the camps were divided with electric barbed wire, Camp A, B, C, D, along with the Gypsy and quarantine camps, and so on. The electrified barbed wire separated each camp with lookout towers with huge searchlights standing on each end of the camp, manned by the SS men. If I had stuck my whole head out, I would have gotten my head shot off. I could not see what was going on, but I was told by the Sonderkommandos that the children were singing while the parents and relatives were burning. People were screaming and yelling, and fire came out from the pits. They burned the corpses while the children were forced to sing and dance; they had to do it. When the screaming silenced down, the same children were pushed into the same pits to be burned alive.

Auschwitz was built on twenty-seven square miles surrounded by swamp. When you go back now, you would never know it was swamp. The swamp was filled with bones and ashes.

A few days later, we were transferred to a neighboring camp. This was Camp D, a working camp. We did not know what kind of work we were going to be doing; all we knew was that we were going to work. This camp had about twenty barracks, each built to hold fifty-two horses. I was told that there were about 30,000 people inside this camp. I never counted the people, but there were two levels of bunks with two or three people sleeping in each narrow bunk. It was very, very crowded. When one person in the bunk turned over, everyone had to turn over, because we were packed together like sardines.

Each morning, we had to get up very early for a roll call. This took a long time, and we had to stand in a straight line. When the guards were satisfied that everyone was accounted for, we were given our breakfast of synthetic coffee and a small slice of bread, which sometimes had mold growing on it. We didn't know it at the time, but this bread actually helped us in some ways, because it gave us a form of penicillin. After we ate our "breakfast," we went to work. Every day, we marched out from camp to work to the sound of the orchestra; we came back to the camp to the sound of the orchestra; we were tortured to the sound of the orchestra. Everything in the camp was done to music.

After many days, the guards came in and took out a large group of people, I was told about 1,800. I don't remember how many *kappos* [a prisoner who acted as foreman] or SS we had marching with us. We marched in lines of four or five people away from Camp D to go to work. They marched us around the camp in a long line to a place every day called the *salegabetrieb* [a scrap yard].

There were cabbage fields along the road where we marched. I was very fast. When we came to a field with cabbage growing, I would step out of line, grab a head of cabbage, and then step back into line. They never caught me. If they had, I would have been killed. The cabbage was being grown for the SS men, not the prisoners. When I got back in line, we quickly ate the cabbage as we walked. On the other side of the cabbage were very long trenches for storing potatoes for the winter. Other prisoners worked putting the potatoes in the trenches and covering them with straw and dirt. They left little openings, which had tubes coming up and were shaped to look like a chimney coming out of the trenches. They were spaced along the trenches containing the rows of potatoes so that the potatoes could get some air. I could not get any potatoes, because this field was too far away.

There was a railroad siding that came into the salegabetrieb, where gondola trains brought in German airplanes that had been shot down; passenger trains traveled outside the scrap yard, on a parallel track going to different cities. These people must have seen what was going on.

My job in the salegabetrieb, since I was very agile, was to be the "rangermaster." This meant it was my job to couple and uncouple the gondola cars from the other cars. After uncoupling the car, I had to go up the steps to the top of the gondola and turn the wheel to apply the brakes. While this was being done, the German air force man was using the train engine to push the cars into different railroad sidings.

My job was not very difficult, but it was very dangerous. I had to be extremely quick and never make a mistake. If I made a mistake, the train wheels would run over me. The Polish engineer brought the trains to the front entrance of Birkenau. At this point, the air force man took over the engine, because the Polish engineer was not allowed to enter Birkenau. When the air force man spotted where the car was supposed to stop, it was my job to make sure the car got to the right spot so the plane could be pushed off the flatcars by the prisoners to the ground to be processed. The plane's motor was removed and the aluminum and stainless steel cut and separated, along with copper, brass and other forms of metal. All of this was done by the prisoners, using axes to cut the aluminum. They later loaded the different metals into open coal cars, to be shipped to mills and make new materials.

Most of the time, the airplanes that came in were German planes, but sometimes a foreign plane was brought in. The prisoners did not like it when this happened, because the foreign planes were made of thicker aluminum than the German planes, making them harder to cut with axes. From time to time, we would hear American airplanes flying overhead. At the moment we heard the planes, the SS let out smoke to cover the entire camp. The SS men blew sirens. We were made to lie on the ground with our faces down and arms spread straight out. As I look back, the only reason I can think of why we had to lie down was to keep us from signaling with a mirror to the "enemy" airplanes.

20

I Become a Partisan

JOINING THE UNDERGROUND IN BIRKENAU, 1944. Some of the airplanes that came into the salegabetrieb still had fuel in their tanks. The fuel had glycerin or something in it. Prisoners would come to the planes, knock a hole in the fuel tank, and drink the liquid. That liquid would make them so high that you could almost see their heads spinning. I remember one day the German air force man saying, "They should not drink that fuel. They will go blind or even kill themselves."

"Why can't they drink this?" I asked.

"Because it's poisonous!" he said, explaining the effects of the chemicals.

I went to the guys who were drinking the fuel and said, "Don't drink that fuel—you will go blind!"

The prisoners didn't pay any attention to me, just went right on drinking the fuel. Some of the prisoners went blind; others died. The prisoners didn't care. For the moment, they were happy and could forget where they were. At this point, I decided to take a sharp piece of metal and make holes in the fuel tanks before the planes were pushed into the salegabetrieb. Even though I did this, those tanks still dripped fuel. I could see the other prisoners gathering around those tanks to catch whatever they could, just to feel happy for a little while and forget their pain.

Sometimes the trains brought in other things besides the shot-down airplanes. One time there was a railroad car filled with potatoes, which was supposed to stay outside the work area. I left the "potato" car attached, and the engineer pushed it inside along with the rest of the railroad cars carrying the airplanes. I told the other guys that I knew where I had left the car. They went over, crawled through the windows, and threw out the potatoes to the other people, who were waiting outside.

The work group I was assigned to had thirty people, including Russian prisoners of war. The Russian prisoners ranked from lieutenant to general, but the generals did not go to work. I was the only little Jewish boy in this work unit. The kappo in charge was a political prisoner from Austria. At one point, the Russian prisoners came to me and asked me to tell them which airplanes had machine guns in their wings. I started pointing out to the Russians the planes with guns in their wings and never thought anything more about it.

I continued doing my job as rangermaster, coupling and uncoupling the railroad cars. I did this every day. When we were finished, I used to go sit inside the train engine room with the air force man and feed coal into the fire to keep the water hot. The trains in Birkenau ran on steam, so we had to keep the water hot all the time.

One winter day, I decided to go into the kappo's little tent to eat my soup, where it would be a little warmer. When I went inside, I saw some of the Russian prisoners holding something that I didn't like. I turned around very quickly to go back outside, but they called me back. "What did you see?" the Russians asked me.

"You were just playing with some steel," I answered.

One of the Russians held out the gun he had been holding and asked, "Does this look like just a piece of steel to you? Now you are in the underground, you are one of us."

After I saw what the Russians were doing with the machine guns taken from the planes, I had no choice, knowing that I could be in more danger, and I agreed to become a member of the underground in Auschwitz-Birkenau.

As a member of the underground, I became a leader with four other people. I knew who my four people were, and I knew the other leaders, but I didn't know the people under the other leaders, just as they didn't know who was under me. In the underground, we all took an oath that if any one of us were caught, we would never reveal who else was in the underground. Not knowing the other people involved was added protection, so that if we were tortured, we couldn't tell.

I finally understood why the Russians had asked me to point out the planes with the machine guns on them. The Russians were taking the machine guns out of the wings of the planes and remaking them into smaller handguns that could be smuggled back into camp. Every day, someone different was "chosen" to be the gun carrier. I remember the day I was "chosen" for gun carrier duty.

We never knew when we went back to camp from work if the SS were going to search us, or if we were just going to be counted as we walked by. Often, many days would pass before the SS would conduct a search. On the day I was carrying the gun, everyone was being searched. There was a long line of people ahead of me. I could not show any fear. I had the gun in my pants, hidden between my legs. I knew that if I got caught with this gun, I would have been immediately shot.

There were about two hundred people ahead of me in line still waiting to be searched. I could see my friends as they went through. I was not scared; I had a feeling something was going to happen. When there were about three people ahead of me in line, a bunch of guys on the other side of me started pushing and pulling each other, creating a distraction, on purpose. The SS started beating and whipping the guys with their bullwhips. During the shuffle, I was pulled to the other side of the group and blended in with the people who had already been searched. I turned around, just like nothing had happened, and all of a sudden, things settled back down. When the search was finished, we took a loaf of bread, put the gun inside, and threw the bread over the fence to the Sonderkommando working in the crematorium. There were many people involved in the underground. There was a Polish lady who worked in the SS headquarters. She would smuggle out picture negatives, hoping that someone would see what was happening and come to liberate us. I never met this lady, because everything was very secretive. The SS must have been watching her. One day when we came back into camp from work, the orchestra was playing as usual. The gallows had been set up in the open space between the gates of the camp and the barracks. Three people, two men and a woman, were standing under the gallows on chairs with nooses around their necks, and the Polish woman was one of them.

As we walked into the area, we were given an extra slice of bread. We then had to go around the gallows, looking at the three people standing on the chairs. As we passed by, the SS would yell, *"Augen rechts!"* which means, "Eyes to your right!" Then we had to take a bite of the bread. It was as if the SS were trying to show us, "Don't you ever try something like this!"

As we passed by the three people, we could see they had been tortured and beaten. Their ears were hanging down; they were bloodied, and we could see the black and blue marks on them. Their tongues were hanging out of their mouths. I looked at them and said to myself, "They did not talk." Right then, the SS men kicked the chairs out from under their feet. The SS left them hanging out in the open on the gallows for a long time. At curfew, some of the other prisoners took them down from the gallows and took them to the crematorium. I was glad they didn't talk, because there would have been plenty of people who would have gone with them to their deaths, including me.

I was told that the underground had a plan. There was going to be an uprising in Auschwitz. The little group I was in charge of was going to participate by fighting with whatever we could find or by catching one of the SS men. I was told that some of the Sonderkommando had been able to get weapons from the SS guards by going to the watchtowers with gold watches they had gotten from Kanada, the area in the camp where prisoners gathered all food, clothes, and valuables. They then took them to a warehouse to be separated and stored.

The Sonderkommando would call up to the guard in the tower and say, "Hey, isn't this a beautiful watch?"

The guard would look down from the tower and say, "Why don't you throw it up?"

One of the prisoners on the ground would then say, "Oh no, if I throw it up and you miss, it will be damaged. Why don't you come down here?" Not knowing what was going on, the guard would then come down from the watchtower to look at the watch. This is when the Sonderkommando would get behind the guard and cut his throat. Other prisoners told me that in this way, the prisoners were able to get the guard's machine gun to use in the uprising and have a better chance of escaping.

Now, no one knew exactly when the main uprising was going to happen. However, the Sonderkommando found out that they were all going to be sent to the gas chambers. On October 7, 1944, the uprising began in Birkenau. The uprising was supposed to start simultaneously in Auschwitz and Birkenau; but when the Sonderkommando in Birkenau found out they were going to die in the gas chambers, they decided to begin the uprising in order to fight the Germans and die with dignity.

The uprising looked just like a war. German tanks were all over the place. Everyone in the Sonderkommando was killed. During the fighting, the Sonderkommando managed to destroy one of the crematoria and one of the gas chambers. Lots of people didn't know what was going on during the uprising, but they heard the shooting and knew something was happening. Then, as quickly as it started, the uprising was over. The uprising lasted only an hour, two hours at the most. After the uprising, they watched us very closely. We didn't have any more uprisings. It was like cutting off the wings from your own body; you can do absolutely nothing anymore.

All this time, the transports continued to bring people into Auschwitz-Birkenau. Because I worked in the salegabetrieb, I could see the people inside the boxcars. I had to uncouple and separate the boxcars with the people in them from the flatcars with the airplanes on them. As I walked around the boxcars, the people would call out from the little window, "Where are we?" I could not answer their questions. I was not allowed to say anything, and I never knew where the SS men were. Sometimes when the trains came into camp, there were lots of SS men on them, although the SS stayed in the little observation area on the trains. Even though I couldn't say anything, I tried to show with my facial expressions that something was wrong.

21

Tomorrow Will Be a Better Day

DREAMING OF FREEDOM IN BIRKENAU, 1944. Seeing everything that was going on in the concentration camp was very, very hard on me. I was always making notes in my head. I knew that someday I was going to be free and would tell my story. I always said, "They can torture my body, but they can never kill my spirit. I am a free person, and I will survive."

I was always dreaming and fantasizing about freedom and talking to my friends, trying to lift their spirits. I remember one evening, we were all standing around outside before curfew. I looked up at the sky. I said to them, "Hey guys, do you see the beautiful stars shining on us? Look to your left and you have dark clouds." And I stopped.

The guys asked, "And that's all?"

And I said, "Tomorrow." We then went back to the barrack.

The next day, we walked out to the same place. The guys said, "Uh-oh, Mike is going to tell us another story."

I said, "Remember the beautiful stars and the dark cloud? Those stars were traveling slowly and pushed away the dark clouds. Now, everything is shining over us. Tomorrow is going to be a better day." That's how I used to uplift their spirits, by telling stories.

Other times, we stood outside watching birds flying in, picking at the ground. The birds were free—we were not. I watched those birds flying in and out, never staying too long on the ground, because people would catch them, tear them apart, and eat them. I always asked myself, "What can they pick that we cannot see?" I turned to my friends beside me. "Take a look at the birds," I said. "They are coming and going; nobody is asking what they are doing over here. Nobody is asking for any identification—they are free. I think I am going to change myself into a bird."

As I walked away, my friends said, "Mendel, you are crazy." I didn't pay any attention to them. I went inside the barrack, lay down on the bunk, and closed my eyes. I fantasized that I was a bird, and I flew out! I said to myself, "I am going to fly all over the world." The world was so beautiful! When I opened my eyes, I was again in the same surroundings; but for those few moments, I was free. It was a tremendous feeling!

A few days later, we were again standing outside, where we could see railroad cars traveling up and down the tracks. There were boxcars and flatcars on the tracks. I told my friends, "Take a look at how freely the train moves on the track. I think I'm going to change myself into a plank of wood and be part of a passenger car and travel." I left my friends.

As I walked away, they said, "Mendel is getting off his rocker." They thought I had lost my mind.

I went inside the barrack, again lay down on the bunk, and closed my eyes. I pretended that I changed myself into a plank of wood and became part of a railroad car. I was part of the passenger car and looked out the window as I traveled on the train. I traveled all over the world. I could see people walking and children playing with their fathers and mothers, smiling and laughing while they were picnicking—it was so beautiful! I was again free and could forget my problems for those few moments. When I opened my eyes, my friends were all standing around, looking down at me. "Why are you grinning so?" they asked. "What makes you so happy?"

I looked up at them. "Guys, you wouldn't believe it! It was beautiful—I traveled all over the world, I was free!"

Dreaming of freedom is really what kept me going. It was

very important that I never let the things that were happening around me get to me. If I did, I was a dead person. I knew I was alive and that I would survive as long as they didn't push me into the gas chambers or shoot me. I always kept my hope and my belief. I always thought positive. To my friends I said, "Always think positive—not negative. Tomorrow will be a better day."

Other people in the camp would ask, "How could God let this happen to us?" These people gave up their faith, and when they did, their armor fell down completely. For me, no matter how bad things were, I always kept my faith. I remember lying on my bunk and closing my eyes. I would dream of having a little conversation with God. I was arguing with God about this and that.

I remember one time I opened my eyes and I had a smile on my face. My friends looked at me and said, "Hey, what are you so happy about?"

"You wouldn't believe it," I told them. "I had the biggest arguments and discussions with God."

My friends just looked at me. "Come on," they said, "God wouldn't listen to you anyway."

"Look," I answered, "God did listen to me, because I poured out my heart, and you can see I'm still over here. If I poured my heart out to you people, you would not listen, because we have the same troubles and problems. If I poured out my heart to the SS, I would get killed. So you see, God is the only one who will listen to me." I always had the best feelings after my discussions with God. I felt so relaxed and good. I was far away and free!

From the beginning of the war, we were not allowed to pray in our synagogues, nor were we allowed to pray when we were placed in the concentration camps. One day, in October or November, most of the religious people were praying very quietly, pointing themselves to the east, which is traditional in Judaism, in order to face Jerusalem. Even the non-Jewish people sometimes knelt between the bunks and prayed, especially on Sundays.

I never paid too much attention, but I remember one man in particular, kneeling and praying. I think he must have been Catholic; he had a rosary in his hands. I don't know how he got it, maybe from some of his friends. He might have even been a priest. All of a sudden, while he was praying, the SS commandant in charge of our barracks walked in. Everyone gathered around the man, mingling and talking as if nothing was happening. The people closed in around him, and those closest to him begged, "Please get up—the commandant is here."

The man didn't get up. He was so deep in his prayers that he either didn't hear or didn't care. The commandant got suspicious. Usually when he came in the barrack, everyone scattered in different directions; but this time, they stayed where they were. The commandant, with his club in his hands, pushed everyone aside until he came to the middle of the barrack, where the man was praying. The commandant told the man to get up. I can still see it like it was today; the man never raised his head. The man was holding his hands closed over the rosary, still praying. The SS man started screaming at the man to get up. When the man didn't move, the SS man beat him to death with his club. The SS never had to have a reason to torture or beat us. They were very sadistic in every kind of torture they performed. I remember a man taken out of our barrack for no reason. He was taken to Block 11, stretched face down across a table, and told he was going to get fifty lashes with their bullwhip. They told him to count as the hits came down. If he messed up the counting, the blows would start over. The SS began the beating, and he started counting, "1 . . . 2 . . . 3 . . . 4 . . . 5 . . . 10 . . ." He missed his counting, and they began beating him all over again. By the time they were finished, his back was covered with terrible wounds. After they were done, the SS poured salt all over his back. The man screamed in pain because the salt was burning him to death. The SS walked away, and we took him back to the barracks. We tried to wash the salt out of his back, but he died.

No one could escape the beatings from the SS. An SS man who liked to kill people always stood in front of the gate going into the salegabetreib. He was the one who stood at the gates to make sure no one escaped. This SS man was very sadistic and would kick the men in the place where it hurts the most, right between their legs. When we were standing in line, he would walk a full circle around us until he finally picked someone. Standing in front of the man he picked, he kicked him in the groin. Typically, the man would fall on his knees because of the pain.

The guard then pushed the man over on his back and slowly put his heavy boot on the man's forehead. He would very, very slowly start pushing down on the face while moving his foot slowly down the man's face from his forehead to his chin. He stopped at the man's throat, where he started pushing down slowly. We could see the tongue coming out of the mouth and the eyes filling up with blood. Finally, the man would die.

The SS man beat me, too. One day, he picked me out, stopped in front of me, and kicked me. I don't know if it took a second or a minute or even a hundred years, but I knew what was coming. I closed my eyes and waited. At the moment I felt the movement of his foot toward me, I pulled my stomach in tight and locked my knees as he kicked. When he saw I did not go down on my knees, he walked away. That's the way I had to live day in and day out as a teenager, not knowing from one day to the next if I would be alive.

I never went down on my knees, because I didn't want to give him the satisfaction of killing me. If I had gone to my knees, he would have killed me with his boot on my throat, just like the other men I had seen him kick. I could not show any emotions whatsoever. If I had shown any emotions at all, I would have been killed.

The whole time, I felt sorry for others who were hurt and killed, but I could not get emotionally involved. I had to look out for myself and for my friends. I tried to help my friends any way I could, building their morale and sharing what I could organize. Everything I could find, I shared with my friends.

22

I Am Going to Help You

ROMANCE IN BIRKENAU, 1944. I felt that if I could help people, I wasn't going to take advantage of them. I cared about people, I had feelings, and I had to live with myself after everything that happened. I remember one day in camp trading an American ten-dollar gold piece I had gotten from some guys working in Kanada. The guys brought me the gold piece and asked if I could use it to buy some vodka, cigarettes, and bacon. I talked to the Polish engineer that brought the trains loaded with shot-down planes on them to the entrance of Birkenau. As he was not allowed to come into the camp, we always had our beautiful conversations just at the entrance where the German air force man took over.

It took me a little while, but I convinced the engineer to trade the ten-dollar gold piece for 300 cigarettes. I went back to my friends, telling them I traded the gold piece for 100 cigarettes. They were very happy. I made 200 cigarettes on the deal. Thank God no one searched me when I returned to camp. I distributed my 200 cigarettes one by one to the other prisoners. I didn't smoke. I remember like today one guy I gave a cigarette to. He came back a few minutes later and said, "Here is my ration of bread—give me another cigarette."

I looked at him and said, "You are not going to get any more cigarettes from me! If you can give away your piece of bread, you will never get another cigarette from me!"

One day as I walked to my job as rangermaster at the salegabetrieb, I saw an SS man walking behind me. I started walking faster. I had a bad feeling in my stomach that something was going to happen to me, because this SS man stayed very close behind me. When I reached the train, I stepped onto the steps of the train engine. The SS man swung his bullwhip across my face. Blood started pouring out. I turned to look at the SS man, who asked me, "What happened?"

I had to think fast. I knew he would finish me off if I answered "you hit me."

"I slipped and hit my face as I stepped on the locomotive engine steps," I told him.

The SS man looked at me again, then turned and walked away. When I wiped the blood from my eyes, I told myself, "I'm okay, I have my eye." I was afraid I had lost it.

The German air force man who I worked for at the salegabetrieb asked, "Why did he do that to you?" I suppose he felt sorry for what the SS man had done to me.

Since I worked with aluminum, I fashioned six clamps to use to stop the horrible bleeding from where the bullwhip had dug into my skin. I bent the aluminum clamps in a U-shape with sharp points. I went to a friend and asked, "Will you please put three clamps below and three clamps above my eye?" My friend didn't want to do it, because it would hurt. "It's not going to hurt you, it is going to hurt me," I told him. "Why don't you just hold the clamps in place so that I can clamp them to my skin to close the wound, because I can't see it." I fastened three clamps below and three clamps above my eye as my friend held the skin closed.

The SS people had a routine of checking people back into the camp when we returned from our work duties. While the orchestra was playing as we reentered the camp, the SS would point their fingers and write down the number of anyone who came into the camp injured. In the evening after we were given our rations, the SS men came into the barracks, called out the number of the injured person, and that person was never seen again. When I came close to the gate, I pretended to wipe my face like I was sweating. If they had seen I was injured, I would have been pointed out, and I would not be here today to tell the story. I believe somebody upstairs looked over me that I should survive to tell it.

I remember one day after the uprising. I don't remember the exact day—in camp a day was a month, and a month was like a year. To the side of Camp D was another camp, where the Gypsies used to be. One day when I came back from work, the camp was empty because all the Gypsies had been taken out and sent to the gas chambers. The SS men brought in a bunch of women from the hospital in the women's camp into this Gypsy camp, because the hospital had become overcrowded. When I came back from work that day, I saw a bunch of men walking up and down by the fence. Since it was before curfew, I decided to go over to the fence and see what was going on. I walked up and down the fence, hoping I might see some friends from Konin, or maybe one of my sisters or a cousin. I knew they had all gone to Treblinka—I thought maybe a few had been picked out and sent over to Auschwitz-Birkenau.

I went over to the fence every day after I finished working, hoping to see someone I knew. One day, I saw a girl about my age walking up and down on the other side of the fence. I called her over to the fence. Her head was completely shaved. "What are you doing over here?" I asked.

"There were too many people in the women's camp hospital. Since there were empty barracks in the Gypsy camp, the SS brought us here," she told me.

"Where are you from?" I asked.

"Lodz," she said.

"I am going to help you," I told her. I took out a package of cigarettes from my pocket and threw them over the fence. She reached down and picked up the cigarettes. I said to the girl, "When you go back into the barrack, give the *Blockeltester* [woman in charge of the barrack] a few cigarettes. Now, this is very important: Don't let her see the whole package. Give her five, no more. Tell her you will get some more from a friend tomorrow."

I told her this for a reason. When the SS came in for selections, if they pointed her out, the blockeltester would tell the SS, "No, you can't have her. She is a good worker. I need her right now," because the blockeltester knew she could get more cigarettes from the girl the next day. Cigarettes were hard to get and were an extremely valuable commodity.

I began helping her in other ways, too. I would throw over bread, cigarettes, and even salami when I could get it. One day, I looked down at her feet and saw she had on wooden shoes like they wore in Holland, which were very difficult to walk in. I went to the blockeltester in my barracks and said, "I need some women's shoes. I'll give you a package of cigarettes for them." He brought out a pair of shoes. They were "grandma shoes," the high-topped kind with the laces going all the way up.

I took those shoes over to the fence and tossed them to her. These shoes began a tremendous romance. Every day, I couldn't wait to come back into camp to meet her at the fence. We could never touch. An electrified barbed wire fence separated us, but that didn't stop our romance. It is very hard to explain the feelings I had for her. It was so difficult being in camp—never knowing from one day to the next if I was going to survive, or if I was going to see her the next day.

One day I told her, "Let's have a romance and pretend that we are not in this camp. Let's dream that we are walking in the park holding hands. Now we are sitting on the bench, and now we're coming home." The feelings were so beautiful! The next day, I couldn't wait to come back from work, go to the fence, and see her. Again we went to the park, but this time we were sitting under a tree. The leaves were making music and the birds were singing. Everything seemed so real, I completely forgot that I was in camp!

The next day we met at the fence and began talking about when we were free. We promised to find each other, get married, and begin a new family. I knew I could never hold her in my arms, but it was beautiful—it was my fantasy to hold her in my arms. We met this way day in and day out until we were separated by the Death March. I believe this romance kept us going, since we never knew from one day to the next what was going to happen. I could still share my feelings with someone, even being in that terrible place. I can still see her face today.

23

I Kept Moving My Legs

THE DEATH MARCH, DECEMBER 1944–JANUARY 1945. Some of the SS men lived with their families across from the Birkenau camp. There were buildings in Birkenau that had big red crosses painted on their roofs. A friend of mine in the underground was assigned to a work group that cleaned the area daily, including sweeping the buildings and cutting the grass. He told people in the underground, who told me, "The buildings with the red crosses are not a hospital complex; they're being used for ammunition storage." We got word out to the resistance, who notified England about the buildings being used for ammunition storage.

On Christmas Day, we could see planes flying low overhead in a "V" formation. The Nazis released a smoke screen over the camp. Rumor was that the Americans flew by day and the English by night. The Nazis gathered us in one place where we were working. We had to lie face down on the ground with our hands stretched out over our heads. We heard tremendous explosions. Bombs fell into camp. One bomb fell into Camp A. Another bomb fell across the camp, but neither exploded. I guess God was watching over us that day—hundreds of prisoners would have been killed if either of the 500-pound bombs had exploded.

After the bombing, the Nazis marched us back to camp. We were singing Russian songs as we marched, we were so happy, and there were many Russian prisoners with us. The SS men were outraged at our singing. They screamed at the head kappo, who happened to be a German prisoner, yelling, "How can you let them sing when our German SS soldiers are being killed?" The SS beat the kappo with their bullwhips. The SS were so angry that we didn't get any food that night. We really didn't care; our stomachs were so full of joy that we forgot our hunger.

In January 1945, we knew that the war was coming to an end. The Russians were coming and the Nazis were losing. Most of the Nazis had already run away. On January 18, all the prisoners were gathered up from Birkenau and taken over to Auschwitz, the main camp. We waited there until someone said we were all going to leave. It was around one o'clock in the morning before I actually left Auschwitz. Some of my friends argue with me today, saying it cannot be that we left on the 19th. My answer to them is always, "Maybe you left on the 18th, but I was in the back of the line. I left on the 19th."

I was told that there were 60,000 prisoners who left Auschwitz-Birkenau on January 18–19, 1945. They made us march very fast. We covered thirty-five kilometers, about twenty-one miles a day, in the snow and cold of the mountains of Silesia. Even though most of the snow was hard-packed, it was very difficult to walk on. In some places the snow was soft, and we would sink down into it. I was lucky, because I had civilian shoes and they stayed better on my feet. People with wooden shoes had a very difficult time walking. Sometimes their feet would break through the top of the snow and get stuck. When this happened, they had to stop, pull their shoe out of the snow, and put it back on their foot. Sometimes they fell behind if they sat down to put their shoe back on. The SS men shot those that fell behind. Others were too weak and could not walk anymore; they also gave up and fell behind. The SS men shot them, as well. These people were killed not with straight bullets, but dumdum bullets. Dumdum bullets have the ends cut off, so when the SS shot a person, their head split into pieces. Thousands of people were killed with these bullets. The snow on the side of the road wasn't white, but red with the blood of the prisoners and their split heads.

The whole time we were marching, I remembered the girl I helped in the Gypsy camp. I kept looking for her grandma shoes on the side of the road. I didn't want to find the shoes, but I wanted to know if she survived the march. I never saw those grandma shoes, so I could only hope that she was all right.

At one point, soon after leaving Auschwitz on the Death March, all of a sudden the Nazis made us get off the road, go into a field, and lie down. We heard shooting. When the shooting stopped, they made us go back to the road and continue marching.

We marched for days. We would come into a little town and stop for the night. Some of the other prisoners would sleep in a barn; the rest of us had to sleep outside in the cold. Finally, after several days of marching, we came to a city that had a railroad station. There were open coal cars waiting for us. The SS men packed us into these cars one over the other, like wood, until we were packed very tightly. We could not sit or move very much. We stood shoulder to shoulder, and it was actually warm because of the body heat. The snow blew over us as the train traveled. We didn't have very much food at all, but we had plenty of water— snow. We just scooped it off the backs of the others to drink.

We traveled in the coal cars for several days. Who knows how long—we didn't have a calendar! We traveled from a city in Poland to Vienna, Austria. When we came into Vienna, the SS men began singing, *"Wien, Wien, nur du allein"* [Vienna, Vienna, you're the only one]. They were very, very happy to be in Vienna. We didn't stay long in Vienna, but traveled west to Linz, Austria, and then on to a small railroad station on a hill. We stepped out of the coal cars and had to walk up a very icy, steep hill. The people with wooden shoes couldn't make it up the hill; they kept sliding back down. When they fell behind, the SS men shot them. At the top of the hill was the entrance to the Mauthausen concentration camp.

When the Death March began, I was told 60,000 prisoners left Auschwitz at the same time I did. When we marched into the Mauthausen concentration camp, I was told that there were 24,000 people left. Over 36,000 people from Auschwitz died on the Death March from exhaustion, starvation, or being shot by the SS.

The first thing that happened when we walked into Mauthausen, we were herded into the showers. Hot water came out. The water felt so good, because our bodies were frozen from being outside in the cold for so long. We walked out of the shower and waited for clothes. We never got them. We had to walk completely naked into a small barrack—approximately 400 of us packed into this room. We slept on the floor head to foot, foot to head, like sardines. There was no heat in this room. We stayed warm because of the body heat from the other people. We slept this way until the next morning.

The SS men woke us and made us go outside for roll call—completely naked. We had to stand at attention without moving. It was terribly cold—ten to fifteen degrees below zero centigrade. Some of the people died right there, frozen like icicles. If they saw you moving, the SS would clobber you to death. I said to my friends, "Let's hit each other."

My friends said, "You're crazy—if they see us hitting each other, they will clobber us to death."

I said, "I'm not going to freeze like an icicle and die."

I used to be a good gymnast, and I moved my feet back and forth in the snow. They could never see my upper body move. My movements kept my blood circulating and kept me warm. I was determined not to give the SS men the satisfaction of seeing me die. I kept moving my legs. When the SS men came close, I stood at attention. When they walked away, I rubbed my feet in the snow again to keep warm.

One night the SS commandant came into the barrack and said, "Everybody get up!" We all got up. I thought to myself, "We're in trouble now." We could hear bombs being dropped and knew that someone was very close to camp. I thought they were going to take us out and kill us. "Everyone get up!" the commandant yelled. "You are sleeping too comfortably! I want everyone at the wall to sit down, stretch your legs, and now you will sleep sitting up between each others' legs."

The latrine was at the other end of the barrack. When we had to use the facilities, we had to step on the people who were on the floor. Everyone was yelling, but what choice did we have? There were some clothes on a shelf in a storage area in the latrine. However, the shelf was behind bars. When I went to the latrine, the man who watched to make sure we did our business right was asleep. I saw the clothes and very quietly reached up and gently pulled some down. I was very lucky—I pulled out a shirt and a pair of pants. Quickly, I put the clothes on and returned to the other side of the barrack.

In the morning, the blockeltester came in and said, "People with clothes will go to the kitchen to bring food to the barracks." Some of the prisoners who had been in camp before we got there had clothes. I raised my hand and went to the kitchen for the soup. When I came back from the kitchen I told my friends, "Come first in the line, and when you are finished with your soup, get back in line to get more soup. When you come back a second time, I won't pay attention. If anybody says anything, I'll say, 'I don't know what you're talking about.'" I was always sharing everything with my friends. I never kept things only for myself.

24

It Didn't Make Any Difference What Time It Really Was

Going to Gusen II and becoming a machinist, January–April, 1945. Having clothes gave me the privilege of sleeping on a bunk instead of on the barrack floor. The blockeltester in charge of the barrack had his own room where he slept. Those of us with clothes, who worked in the barrack, slept on a bunk near the blockeltester's room. There was a locker in the blockeltester's room where he kept the extra bread he acquired. At night, after everyone was asleep, I would go to the locker, open it very quietly, and take some bread. Still good at organizing, I took the bread back to my friends and shared it with them. "Eat it quick before anyone sees," I told them.

One morning the blockeltester said, "Someone is stealing bread." Nobody said anything, so the blockeltester set a trap in the locker to catch the "thief." He put a bunch of spoons in the top of the locker so that when the locker was opened, the spoons would fall out, making a lot of noise, and he would wake up. I watched him make this trap, so I knew what to expect. When I opened the locker that night, I was ready to catch the spoons.

Those spoons never made a sound, and he never found out who was stealing—"organizing"—the bread.

A few weeks after arriving in the Mauthausen concentration camp, we were sitting in the barrack when the SS commandant came in. "What professions do you have?" he asked.

I was never a machinist in my life, but I instinctively figured that they were looking for machinists, so that machinists would have a better chance of survival. I quickly raised my hand and said, "I am a machinist."

Days later, the SS commandant returned to the barrack and said, "All machinists report!"

We reported to the commandant, they gave out uniforms, and we walked to another camp. This camp was a sub-satellite camp with ten or twelve thousand people in it. The camp was called Gusen II.

In Gusen II, we were given a loaf of bread for eight people. I used to divide the loaf. When I cut the bread, it was hard to get all the pieces exactly the same size. One piece was always bigger and one always smaller. I remember like today, there was a father and son in my group. When I gave out the bread, I guess one piece was bigger. The son grabbed the bigger piece out of his father's hands and said, "Here is my little piece. You don't need it. I want it to survive."

I was so mad. I couldn't understand. The son was a young man and the father elderly. I told the son, "If I had my father over here, I would not only give him this big portion of bread, I would give him my portion of bread, as well."

I said to myself, "This is not going to happen anymore."

The next day, I cut the bread into eight pieces and I said to a guy, "Turn around. Who should I give this piece of bread to?" In this way, no one would ever know what size the pieces of bread were.

Again we waited several days, until the SS men came and got us, put us in railroad boxcars, and we traveled. We didn't know where we were going until we stopped in front of a mountain. Stepping out of the boxcars, a door opened up leading to one of the tunnels underneath the mountain. These tunnels were miles long and going in different directions. We walked inside one of the tunnels. These tunnels were beautiful! There was a factory inside this mountain. I'm sure the Allies knew these factories were there, but they were so deep at the base of the mountains, no bombs could go through the mountains to them.

Once inside, they put me in front of a table with a frame and some aluminum sheets. I was given a spot-welder and a torch. I looked at them and thought, "What am I going to do with these?" I had never in my life held a spot-welder or torch, but I learned very fast to be one of the best machinists they could find. If I didn't, I would have been dead.

I soon found out what I was making. It was the "shot vant" for the Messerschmidt planes flown by the German air force. The shot vant is the wall dividing the cockpit from the tail of the Messerschmidt plane. My job was to make this part for the back of the plane's fuselage. I spot-welded the aluminum plate to the frame. Then I cut three holes in the plate so that wires from the cockpit could pass through these holes to the back flaps.

Either the SS man or a civilian inspector inspected each completed part. The parts had to be right every time. The holes had to be cut exactly on the place marked on the aluminum plate and the plate welded very tightly to the aluminum frame. I did this job day in and day out. This factory was a long distance from Gusen II, and we always traveled by train. When we left the factory in the afternoon, I tried to be in one of the first boxcars so that I could be first in line for soup, hoping that I could go get back in line for seconds. I was always one of the first people in line to get the soup.

One day, as I was sitting spot-welding and cutting the aluminum, a guy came up to me and said, "Move." I picked up my chair and moved. Again he said, "Move" I moved my chair back to where it was originally. I thought he was a kappo without an armband. Finally, he said, "I don't want you to move your chair, I want you to move those holes."

I looked at him and said, "You're crazy. If I move those holes and they measure it, I'm going to get shot right here." He walked away, and I continued with my work.

The next day he came back to my table and said, "I know who you are."

"What do you mean?" I asked cautiously.

"You're one of us," he answered.

"Sure," I said, "I'm a prisoner just like you."

"Oh, no," he said, "News travels very fast. We know you were a part of the uprising at Auschwitz-Birkenau, on October 7, 1944, but you did not participate," he told me.

During the whole time this guy was talking, I was thinking, "He knows too much about me; he must be a part of the underground." I had to make a decision. I decided to take a chance.

"Why do you want me to move these holes?" I asked.

"If you move these holes," he said, "then the cables that come from the front of the cockpit through these holes to the back flaps can't move the flaps. If the holes are not in the right spot, then the pilot will have a hard time moving the flaps to slow down the plane, and the plane will crash."

I thought about what he said and decided to trust him and take part in sabotaging the Messerschmidt planes.

I built one of the shot vants the right way, spot-welding it very tightly and cutting the holes exactly in the place marked. After the shot vant had been inspected as correct, I placed it against the wall. Once the inspectors walked away to check other parts, I did not spot-weld so tightly, and I moved the holes in different directions. When I placed this faulty shot vant against the wall, it was gone in a few seconds. Other prisoners knew what was going on, and collectively we were all sabotaging the airplanes. The other prisoners were replacing the good walls with the bad walls when the planes were being assembled.

One day, I was working as usual when I saw the SS, the *Luftwaffe* people [members of the German air force] and some civilian engineers running up and down the aisles. I thought, "Now we are really in trouble," because I knew the war was coming to an end. I thought, "They're going to take everybody out like we are going to work, put us in an unfinished tunnel, close the entrance, dynamite the tunnel, and we'll all suffocate." We could hear explosions from the airplanes bombing the surrounding cities and the cannons firing. I kept working at my station as if nothing was happening, but all the while kept watching out of the corner of my eye to see what was going on.

Soon the commotion ended, and I saw the guy who told me to move the holes in the shot vant. "Hey, what's going on?" I asked.

"They are checking the aluminum plates, looking for stress fractures in the aluminum for the fuselages of the Messerschmidt planes," he said. "They are not flying; they are crashing." Leaning closer to me, he said, "There are no stress fractures in the aluminum making those planes crash. You had a part in it, and so did other people. Those planes are going up, but the pilots cannot control the flaps to slow down the planes, and the planes are crashing."

I had such a good feeling. We were the ones causing the planes to crash. In a way, we were helping the Allies win the war.

Every camp I was in assigned me a different number. They tried to take away our names and make us just a number. The last number assigned to me was "118860." I saw the SS men, the air force people, and civilians wearing watches. I said to myself, "I'm going to make me a watch to tell time." Since I worked with aluminum, I took a small piece of aluminum and designed the body of my make-believe watch. As I had a little hacksaw, a drill, and a file for working with aluminum, I also made a screw from the aluminum, which I fastened to the side of the watch to make the stem. I put my Mauthausen concentration camp number, 118860, and my initials, "MJ," on the face of my watch. When I looked at my watch, I could tell time. It didn't make any difference what the time was; I knew I had a brain, my brain was working. I knew I had a name, not only a number. I then found some straps, which had holes in them and had been used to fasten wires and keep them together in the fuselage. I took the straps, cut them down, and fastened them to the body of my watch. I kept my watch hidden, as I could have been killed if the SS men had found it. If they ever caught me with my watch, I would be dead—I used their aluminum to make it.

I still have my precious watch. In my mind, my watch has never stopped running. It never missed a second. I don't have to wind it, and it still runs. When I speak to students and let them put my watch to their ears and listen, many of them think they hear it still ticking.

I had one wish—I dreamed that someday I was going to be free. The Nazis could torture and starve my body, but they could never kill my spirit. No matter what they did to me, I still had hope and belief that I would survive. I was always dreaming of freedom. In Mauthausen/Gusen II, I dreamed that someday I was going to have a room with a table, a white tablecloth with a loaf of bread on it, a sharp knife, and a chair. The table would sit in the middle of the room, and when I would get up and move away from the table, there would be no walls surrounding me. When I walk away, I am free!

The white tablecloth reminded me of my family on Friday nights, when we were sitting together at the table; praying together, laughing, crying, and singing together—that's exactly what we did. I dreamt I could cut all the small pieces of bread my heart desired, eat as much as I wanted, and nobody could tell me to stop. I never had enough bread in all those long years. Because I was dreaming, my friends thought I was crazy, but this is what kept me going. I had to dream in order to survive.

25

I Have Waited So Long to Hear That Beautiful Song

LIBERATION AT MAUTHAUSEN/GUSEN II, MAY 1945. We had been in Mauthausen/Gusen II about four months. Around May 1, we started seeing bombs being dropped and hearing the explosions. We knew the war was coming to an end. The thought in all our heads was, "Are we going to make it?" We still rode the trains to work until the last week before we were liberated. By this time, most of the SS had left, but the militia had been sent in to watch us. The militia was made up of very old Austrians, and if we had been stronger, we could have overpowered them and escaped.

We hadn't been to work in about six days and didn't know what was going on outside the camp. I looked out the window one day and saw tanks painted with white stars passing by. I said, "Hey, guys! Look, the Germans have changed from the swastika to a star." I didn't know at the time what the star meant. I kept looking out the barrack window and saw other tanks on the road with lots of Germans without weapons walking in front of the tanks. Then I realized the Germans were prisoners.

My friends said, "Mendel, why don't you go out and find out who they are?"

I said, "Why me?"

They said, "All of a sudden you're afraid?"

I said, "Okay," and walked out. The camp was below and the streets were on high ground. Once outside, I waved to the tanks with my hands going side to side, hoping the soldiers inside would see me. A soldier came out from one of the tank turrets, waved back, and threw out a bar. I picked it up, and it was a bar of chocolate. I ran into the barrack and yelled, "I have a bar of chocolate. Hey, guys! You'll never guess what they named it—Hershel!" [Hershey]. I took a knife and cut the chocolate into small pieces. I gave all the pieces away to my friends, keeping the last small piece for myself. When I put it in my mouth, I prayed, "God, please don't let it melt too fast." That chocolate was so delicious, I can still taste it.

Looking out the window again, I saw a civilian with a Red Cross armband and a soldier with a machine gun in front of the fence, waving and motioning that someone should come out. I decided to go out again. Approaching the fence, the civilian asked me if I spoke German. "Yes," I said. He told me that I was free. The Americans had arrived, and I needed to stay in this camp. Soon, they were going to come and take everyone back to the main camp of Mauthausen. He said, "We are going to give you food, medicine, everything you want."

I couldn't believe it. Were we actually free? I had waited so long to hear that beautiful song, the beautiful music, those beautiful words that I was free. Now they wanted me to go back to Mauthausen? "I have waited so long to know that nobody in the world can keep me in this camp. I am going to walk out."

As I walked away, the soldier called to me and asked me in German if I spoke Polish. Again, I said, "Yes." Now I got scared, because if he spoke German and Polish, he couldn't be an American, he had to be a *Volksdeutcher*, a German born in Poland. Frightened, I slowly started to move away from him. He called me back, and since he had a machine gun, I had no choice but to come forward again. When I got closer he said, "Don't be afraid. I am from Chicago. My mother is German and my father is Polish. That is why I speak both languages." Then he told me the same thing in Polish that the Red Cross civilian had said in German.

I went back to my friends and told them the Americans had

come and we were free. The Red Cross man said we should stay in this camp and they would take us back to Mauthausen. They would give us food, medicine, and anything we needed.

Even though we were free, there was still no food for us to eat. I remembered that there was a farm across from the camp on a hill. As we rode the train to work everyday, we saw farms all along the railroad tracks. I decided to go to one of the farmers and get a pig or cow, kill it, and bring the meat back to camp to cook. I found a rifle in the camp and went to the farmhouse across from the camp, about one hundred yards away from where the German families lived. I knocked on the door. The door opened, and there stood a woman with her daughter.

"I have come over here to kill a pig. Where is your husband?" I asked. She told me her husband had gone away, and they were alone. I decided he must have been an SS man and ran away because he was afraid the prisoners or the Americans would come after him. I asked, "Did you know what was going on down there in that camp?"

"No," she said, "we saw people going back and forth to work."

"Did you know it was a concentration camp?" I asked. "Thousands of people were dying, hundreds every day, and you never knew anything about it?"

"No, we never knew about it," she said.

I asked if she had any bread, and she brought out a round loaf of sourdough. "I cannot believe you could look over into that camp and tell me you never saw the SS people as they passed by on the train. We traveled this rail every day going to work, while the SS men were feasting and drinking at your house. This was a terrible concentration camp! When the wind blew, could you not smell the death?" I asked her. She didn't answer, just stood there looking at me. I cocked the rifle and said, "Look, I am not the type of person who will take revenge on other people. I still cannot believe you people didn't know what was going on!"

Finally, she spoke. "Yes, we did know the camp was over there and that you were going to work. But what was going on inside the camp, we didn't know about that." Still finding this hard to believe, I left her comment alone.

"Let me tell you something," I said. "You better take your horse and wagon and get out of here."

"How can I?" she asked, "I cannot leave my home."

"Listen, lady, right now you are talking to a nice boy. Take your daughter and leave." I told her. "In about five minutes, the rest of the prisoners are going to be here, and if they find you, you are going to get killed. Killed with hate or worse." The woman got scared, took her daughter, and left with their horse and wagon.

I went to their barnyard and found an old sow. When I shot her, the kick of the rifle on my shoulder made the bullet go up very high and miss. I shot again. This time my aim was good, and she fell to the ground. Suddenly, I heard many people coming into the yard, making a tremendous noise. Quickly, I took my knife and cut a large piece of meat off the pig to take back to my friends. The other prisoners coming into the barnyard quickly began cutting meat off the pig, as well. The meat wasn't kosher, but we didn't care at this point. There were so many people gathered around that pig that no one could see what they were doing. All of a sudden, someone screamed, "I've lost my finger!" In all the excitement of getting some meat, someone had cut off his finger!

I gathered up my piece of meat, left the farm, and returned to camp. We built a fire, found a big pot, and started cooking the meat. I cut the bread into small pieces and gave everyone a portion. As it cooked, that piece of meat smelled delicious! We sat around the fire watching the pot. Somebody was always asking if it was ready yet. They wanted to dip their bread into the pot as the meat cooked. I kept watch on it, saying, "Don't worry about it. When it's ready, we will eat." I watched the meat until it was very, very brown.

I made everyone move back. I took the meat out of the pot and put it on a piece of paper that was on the ground. I turned the pot upside down and let all the fat run out of the pot. As I poured the fat on the ground, the other guys were stunned. If looks could kill, I would have been dead. They shouted, "How can you pour the fat on the ground?"

I turned to them and said, "You will thank me later on, because our stomachs are so shrunken that if we eat any fat, we are going to have lots of problems. Maybe we will get diarrhea or even die."

As I spoke, I cut the meat into very small pieces, each the size of a walnut, and gave them to my friends so they could eat the meat with the bread. When the guys got the meat and bread, they asked, "Is this all we get?"

"Yes," I answered. "Tomorrow you will get another piece, and another the next day, until our stomachs can tolerate more food."

As we were sitting around they said, "Are you playing doctor again?" They said this because when they had cuts or bruises I looked for grease to put on the cuts. If I found no grease I told them to urinate on their wounds because it was sterile.

It really didn't matter what I said to them. They were very angry with me because they wanted to eat more. I never gave in, because of my feeling that our stomachs just couldn't handle solid food. While we were sitting, finishing our food, another guy, who stayed in the same barrack as me, came running up to our group. He was very happy and jumping up and down. "What are you so happy about?" I asked.

"Mendel," he said, "you wouldn't believe the meal I just had. I caught a chicken and cooked it!"

"Well," I asked, "what did you do with the meat?"

"Meat?" he asked, "who needs meat? The chicken fat was so good that I drank it."

I stood there looking at him. "Are you going with us to Linz tomorrow?" I asked.

"Yes," he replied, "but I think I am going to go back to my barrack and lay down after my big meal. I am going to rest and sleep, and nobody can tell me what to do now."

After he left, I turned to my friends and told them I had a feeling this guy was not going to be around tomorrow.

The other prisoners thought I was crazy, but I was proved right when we went over to his bunk the next morning. We went over together, but we couldn't even get close to his bed. I thought he had burst, because everything had come out of him and he died. I turned to my friends and asked, "Now do you see why I didn't want to give you more to eat? Our stomachs cannot handle food, because they are so shrunken."

The same thing was happening all over camp. When the Americans came in and saw the shape we were in, they tried to do whatever they could to help us. They brought in chocolate, bread, and meat—everything they thought we could eat. Prisoners started dying all over, and the Americans couldn't understand why. When the doctors came, they asked the soldiers why so many people were dying after the liberation. "What are you doing for them?" a doctor asked. The soldiers said they were feeding us, and the doctor said, "My God, put them on a diet!" When everyone went on a diet to regulate the amount of food our stomachs could handle, people stopped dying.

On the day we were liberated, May 5, 1945, another friend from the same city as myself, and the same age—we went to school together—came up to me and said, "Mendel, we are free!"

I said, "Yes, Jerzyk, we are free!"

He was looking in my eyes and said, "It's so beautiful that we can go home now."

"Yes, Jerzyk," I said, "we will go home."

Standing in front of me, he suddenly said, "You know, I feel weak and dizzy."

At that moment, he fell into my arms. I held him up. "Jerzyk, Jerzyk," I called. He didn't answer. He died in my arms. I picked him up and carried him to his bunk. I guess he died from the excitement or something, I don't know. It's a shame, because he lived through all the ghettos, the concentration camps, and finally made it to liberation. I don't know—maybe he was already sick. At least he died a free person, not a prisoner.

• • •

A few days after my liberation from Mauthausen/Gusen II, I learned that it was the 41st Tank Battalion of the 11th Armed Division, the Thunderbolts, that liberated us. Thank you for giving me back my freedom.

26

Sister, There is Something Wrong With This Scale

LEAVING MAUTHAUSEN/GUSEN II, MAY 1945. When the Americans arrived at Gusen II, we were told we would be taken back to the main camp of Mauthausen. I told my friends I wasn't waiting to be sent back to Mauthausen; I was leaving. "Mendel is crazy!" they said to one another. "Where are you going to go? What are you going to do? You have no money!"

I looked at them. "I know I don't have any money, but I am leaving, and anyone who wants to come is welcome to go with me." Three of my friends decided to join me. One of them, Lutek Burzynski, was born in Konin. We went to school together and survived the same ghettos and concentration camps.

Walking out of the camp, I stopped for a moment and looked back. I realized that nobody was waiting for me; nobody was waiting to welcome me home. In fact, I had no home to go to. I told myself, "Mendel, you just keep going and think positive." At that moment, we started walking, and I never looked back.

We left Gusen II and started walking to Linz, Austria, about seventeen kilometers, ten miles, away. We had to stay off the main roads because the American Military Police would pick us up and take us back to camp. We walked on side roads and through fields where no jeeps, cars, or trucks could travel. Reaching Linz, we went to a bombed-out building where Catholic nuns were giving out soup. Walking inside, my friends took big bowls of soup, but I only took a little bit. Looking around, I saw a scale and stepped on it to weigh myself.

As I stood on the scale I said, "Sister, there is something wrong with this scale."

She said, "Son, there is nothing wrong with the scale." I stepped off the scale and checked it—nothing was wrong with it.

I stepped back on the scale and said, "Sister, how can this be? I'm nineteen and a half years old, and I only weigh thirty-two kilos [about seventy pounds] on this scale."

After eating our soup, we walked around, looking for a place to live. We found a bombed-out house with a nice room in it. I was told that Italian workers had lived there, but returned to Italy when the war ended. The railroad station was behind the house. Several days later, I went to the main square of the city. I heard that American MPs were gathering Survivors born in Eastern Europe and putting them in displaced persons' camps to be sent home. Coming into the main part of the city of Linz, the soldiers put me on a truck. They could tell I was a Survivor by my haircut, which had a wide cut across the length and middle of my head, which I jokingly called the *Läusen-Strasse* [the Promenade of Lice].

I said to myself, "My God, I'm a free person, and now they're forcing me to go back to Poland? I am free!"

I can still hear the people on the truck crying, "Don't send me back to Russia—I'll be killed!" I didn't hesitate. I jumped off the truck. A soldier with a rifle came up and pointed it at me, motioning for me to get back on the truck. I opened my shirt and said to him, "Shoot—I have nothing more to lose." He just looked at me. I walked away and the truck drove off.

I found another bombed-out building, which had been a bunch of stores with show windows. I went into one of the stores and found a big piece of white paper. I took a pen and wrote, "Any Jewish person who was born in Poland, please come in. Write your name and the city where you were born." I put this sign in the storefront window. A few people came in, signed their names, and wrote down their birthplaces. Some people did not want to sign in, because they were afraid; they were still fearful of signing their names. Others asked me why I was doing this. I explained, "If you sign in and there are hundreds like you, people will check the list. Maybe you will find a father, mother, brother, sister, uncle, or friend. Who knows?" I was hoping to find some of my family still alive. I remember it like today, one man came in and checked the list. He started yelling. I was afraid he was going crazy. I can still hear him. "Oh my God!" he screamed. "That's my father—that's my brother!" This is why I wanted people to sign in.

I went back to the house I was staying in. I guess my friends went to get some food, for at that time Survivors could go into a store, ask for food, and it was given to them. I was sitting outside on the steps. A girl about my age was walking along the sidewalk. When she came closer, I asked her if she would like to sit down and talk. She did, and we had a nice conversation. She asked me why I lived in a bombed-out house. I said I was liberated from the concentration camp, Mauthausen/Gusen II. I told her I was a Survivor. She asked me, "Why?"

"Because I'm Jewish, I said."

"You are Jewish?" she asked, and at the same time her hand went across my forehead.

I said to her, "You are not going to find what you are looking for. You are looking for horns, aren't you? You will not find them."

She said her parents always told her Jews had horns. "They lied to me," she said. She then asked me if I would like to come over for dinner. She lived across the street in a nice house that was never bombed.

When my friends returned, I told them about my nice conversation with the girl who lived across the street. In the evening she was waiting for me in front of her house. We walked into the dining room. It was beautiful! There was a long table with a white embroidered tablecloth, beautiful dishes, and silver. I hadn't seen that for over five and a half years. Supper was served, and as we were eating, the girl said to her mother and father, "He's Jewish; he has no horns."

She kept arguing, "Why did you lie to me? They are like us. Jews don't have horns."

The parents said, "We never told you Jews had horns.

The girl said, "Yes you did, yes you did. Why did you lie to me? Why did you always tell me that Jews had horns? Why did you lie to me?"

I was enjoying my supper while she talked to her parents. When supper was over, she asked me if I would like to come again for supper the next night. I said I would love to. I went back to my house and told my friends that I had a beautiful supper and I was invited back for the next night. The next evening I went back, and as I walked into the dining room I asked her where here father was. She said he left. I asked her why. She said he was a big Nazi and he was afraid to stay.

Finally, a group of Jewish people came to say we were going to be taken illegally to Palestine, as the British who were in control were not allowing Jews to immigrate to Palestine. We were again put in boxcars and traveled to the German city Mittenwald, near the Austrian border. We stepped out of the boxcars in Mittenwald and marched into a former German military camp on the outskirts of Mittenwald. We waited and waited, and nothing happened. I told my friend Lutek Burzynski, "Let's go to the city and see what's going on." We left camp and walked into Mittenwald.

The next day, after again spending the night at the military camp, we returned to Mittenwald. I saw a building occupied by American soldiers and asked if I could help in the kitchen. They said, "Okay." Every morning, Lutek and I walked into Mittenwald; he walked around the city while I worked in the kitchen. At least I had some good food! One evening when we went back to the camp, everyone was gone! We ended up staying in Mittenwald.

As it turned out, quite a few Jewish Survivors were living in Mittenwald. They had been taken out of the concentration camp Dachau and marched to the Austrian border when the American soldiers liberated them on the outskirts of Mittenwald. We found out that some of the survivors lived in the Hotel Traube and others lived in private homes. Lutek and I took a room in the Hotel Traube.

Working in the kitchen for the American soldiers turned out to be a really good thing. After I had worked there a while, the whole company was moved outside of Munich to a place called Flak Kazern, which had been a military base for the Nazis. While I was working in the kitchen, my friend Lutek moved out from the Hotel Traube to a private home and lived with a family. I remained on the base with the soldiers. A few weeks later, the men on the base found out that they would be sent back to the United States because they had enough points allowing them to go home. Before the soldiers left, they gave me food, cameras, clothing, everything they had and didn't want to take home. I took everything back to Mittenwald, moved in with Lutek, and put all the goods in the basement of the house we lived in. We really enjoyed the food and goods. I still have one of the cameras.

Soon I organized a soccer sports club, and we traveled to camps and cities to play soccer with other displaced-persons soccer clubs. I learned that a sports school in Landsberg had been established by Jewish organizations. It was located in a displaced persons' camp. I finally decided to go back to school and get my teaching certificate in physical fitness at the school in Landsberg. The school was called "The Seminar for Sport Instructors." After earning my teacher's certificate, I was asked to join the Jewish Physical Fitness Association in Munich. I was the youngest person in the group. I was then sent to displaced persons' camps and cities to organize sports clubs and teach calisthenics. We don't call it calisthenics anymore. Today it's more sophisticated; we call it aerobics. I went around organizing and teaching until most of the Jews had left for different countries. As I was practicing gymnastics in the German gymnasium, members of the German Sports Club approached me and asked if I would teach the German children gymnastics. I said, "Sure."

They looked at me in a surprised manner.

I said, "What's the matter?"

They answered, "You always tell us that the Nazis killed Jewish children, and now you are willing to teach German children gymnastics?"

I said, "Those German children had nothing to do with it."

My answer came as a big surprise to them. After that, I taught German children gymnastics, until I left for the United States in 1951.

I also participated in track and field events that were held in 1947 in competition with displaced persons in the American, French, and English zones. The event was called the "Maccabiah." I still hold the record in the 100 meters, the 400 meters, and the broad jump. I still enjoy looking at my trophy, photographs, and certificates commemorating the event hanging on the wall in my home.

– 27 –

We Must
Remember

GERMANY, 1945–1951. In Munich after the war, I found some of the women I helped in Birkenau. They came together one day and invited me to their home. They gathered a lot of pillows and placed the pillows in a pile on top of a bed. The women wanted me to sit on top of the high stack of pillows so they could pay me homage like a king. They said I had saved their lives by giving them cigarettes in camp. The cigarettes were very important to them—they were called *Machorka*. The cigarettes were very strong and highly prized. They were able to get bread in trade for the cigarettes. I didn't smoke, so the cigarettes meant nothing to me, but I also used them to organize food to give away because it was important to me to try and save lives.

My cousin Avram, who had been hidden by a Righteous Gentile woman in Ostrowiec, Poland, decided to move to Munich after the war, where he learned that I was alive and living in Mittenwald. He came to visit me and decided to join me in Mittenwald. One day, as we traveled by train to Munich, the train stopped at the Feldafing station, located near the displaced persons' camp. I looked out the window and saw a woman approaching the train, and I said, "My God, that's her!" It wasn't her face that gave her away, but the way she walked. When we were in Birkenau, I always watched her as she walked away from the fence until she disappeared behind the barrack. She came into the same compartment in the railroad car. Usually, I would stand and give a woman my seat, but this time I turned and said to my cousin, "Will you please get up? Let her sit down over here."

He got up, she sat down next to me, and I stared at her, as I had decided it was she. She started to move away from me, saying, "What are you looking at? Why are you staring at me?"

"What camp were you in?" I asked her.

"Auschwitz-Birkenau" she said.

"No, I mean, what was your last camp?" I asked.

"As there were too many women in the hospital in the Birkenau women's camp, they brought many of us to the Zigeuner camp, a Gypsy camp, which had been liquidated," she answered. "I was in that camp."

"You know, you are very familiar to me," I told her. "Let me tell you a story of why I know you. There used to be a guy in Camp D, which was separated from the Gypsy camp by electrified barbed wire. Every day after work, you would meet him by the fence and talk. One day he threw over a package of cigarettes. The next day, he threw over bread, and margarine. Remember, one day he threw over a pair of grandma shoes for you?" I retold the whole story of our romance to her.

"Wouldn't that be nice to meet this guy again?" she asked.

"Why?" I asked.

"You know, he saved my life," she answered. Pointing across the train compartment, she said, "I'm married now; there's my husband. We go to Munich every day to attend the University."

"What would happen if that same guy who helped you in the camp and just told you this story happens to be sitting here next to you?" I asked her. She took a look at me. She jumped up screaming and embracing me. People came running into the compartment from all directions to protect her.

"No, no, he was not a kappo," she shouted. "He saved my life in camp!" Then she asked me, "Why don't you meet my husband?"

I turned to him and said, "Hello."

Just then, the train pulled into the station in Munich. We walked off the train together. She grabbed my arm so hard, I thought it was going to break. I walked with her, and my cousin walked with her husband.

"Mendel, do you remember what we promised each other in camp?" she asked.

"No, I don't," I said.

"Come on, you remember what we promised," she said to me. "If we ever found each other when we got out, we were going to get married. We were going to build a family." She told me she was going to divorce her husband and marry me, because I saved her life and we made that promise.

"Come on," I told her, "That was then, this is now. We said that because at the time, it was the only way to make us feel good—we were fantasizing. Let's think about it," I said.

We changed partners. She walked with Avram, and I walked with her husband. Her husband said to me, "Before we got married, she told me if she found the guy who saved her life, then there will be a divorce. At the time I thought, what are the chances of that happening? They are one in a million that she will ever find this guy."

I laughed and told him, "Don't worry about it. Nothing is going to happen."

"Mendel, where do you live?" she asked me.

"I have no home," I told her, "I am traveling."

"Are you going to come visit me?" she asked.

"Sure," I said.

I never visited her. Several years later, in 1951, I was sitting in a Munich office waiting for my exit papers. I was sitting very nicely and relaxed. Someone started patting me on the shoulders. I turned my head; it was she! "Mendel, I am still waiting," she said. I looked over at her husband. He was white in the face!

I asked what they were doing there. She told me they were waiting for their papers to go to New York. "Mendel, you know what we promised ourselves," she said to me again. "I am still thinking about you."

"I'll tell you something, Tecza," I told her, "I promised myself that I am not settling over here in Germany. I will marry nobody in Germany. When I go to the United States, I am going to settle down. I am going to look you up."

I never saw her here in the States, and I don't want to see her. That was a part of my past, a way to make it through those days. In camp, talking to her, I could fantasize and dream, be outside, and I was free. I was free. I could see the park. I can see it now.

Many years later, in 1992, I returned to Birkenau with a group from Dallas, Texas. I walked to the camp in Birkenau, opened the gate where I was a prisoner, and we walked in. I went to the part of the fence where I used to meet her. All of a sudden, I was speaking to her again, loudly. I could visualize her. I turned around and looked back, and everybody had tears in their eyes; they could see that for a moment I was back in camp again. Later on, they told me they could see me talking to this girl, gesturing with my hands without realizing she wasn't really there. I think that's right. I think I spoke to her. I completely went back to 1944. When I started talking to her, I could think. They asked me what I was throwing to her. "Cigarettes," I said. I relived it. It was really nice. It's hard to explain, but it was a different sort of romance, a romance full of love, of feelings and caring.

• • •

I quickly became accustomed to living in Germany. Aside from teaching and working with sports groups, I skied, played tennis, played bridge, and in about 1949 became a shopkeeper. I sold groceries, wine, and liquor.

After spending almost six years in Germany after the war, I decided to leave and go to the United States. I had to go through a long process to be approved for immigration. I finally reached the last office to receive stamps of approval to move to the U.S. The official, Mr. Taylor, looked at my papers and said, "Oh, you're a track man and a gymnast." I was scheduled to go to New York. He looked at my papers again and said, "You're not going to New York."

I asked the translator, a woman, "Why?"

Mr. Taylor said, "In New York there is a big forest of trees. If you were to go and be in the middle of the forest, you would get lost and not know how to get out. I'm talking about people."

I again asked the translator what he was talking about.

By this time, Mr. Taylor was laughing his head off. "I'm going to send you to the biggest state in the United States," he told me.

I asked the translator, "What's the state?"

Mr. Taylor was still laughing. "Texas," he said.

I still had no idea what he was talking about, but I guessed it was okay.

"When you go to Texas," Mr. Taylor told me, "you are going to have the biggest opportunity. It's a state of seven million people. The only thing you have to do is grasp it, and you're going to have the biggest opportunity. Go home; I'm going to see what I can do." I listened to him, then went back to Mittenwald and waited.

Two months later, I received a letter from Frankfurt, Germany, with my exit papers. "Hey, guys," I told my friends, "I am not going to New York. I am going to Dallas, Texas."

They looked at me. "Mendel, you are crazy! Why are you going to Dallas? Why not New York, Baltimore, Chicago, Philadelphia, where more of the displaced people are going? They speak the language you can understand. You are crazy to go to Texas. Don't you watch the movies? No sidewalks, people coming out of beer joints, shooting each other?"

"Guys, what are you worried about?" I asked. "When I get to Dallas, Texas, I will buy me a horse and saddle and ride, too!"

That was the end of it. The Joint Distribution Committee, an agency of the United Jewish Appeal, was responsible for arranging my passage on a ship that had been converted from a military tanker. The *General Muir* was the name of the ship. On my arrival from Breman to New Orleans, the customs officer was surprised when I opened my wooden suitcase and he saw my soccer uniform, soccer shoes, ski boots, ski sweater, along with a few clothes. I walked outside of the customs area along with others, my name was called, and people from the New Orleans Jewish Community gathered us together. I was picked up by a women who took me to the Jewish Community Center, where I rejoined the other people of the group who were on the ship with me. We showered, and they served us food. I was the only one of the group coming to Dallas. The committee at the center gave me fifteen dollars for expenses and put me on the train to Dallas. I did not know if anyone would be waiting for me at the Dallas train station.

PART III

American Adventure

28

Dallas,
Here I Am

DALLAS, 1951–1984. Arriving in Dallas, I saw people wearing the big hats, and it reminded me of the hat I saw on Mr. Taylor's desk. He must have been a Texan! Thank you, Mr. Taylor, for sending me to Dallas, Texas.

When I came to Dallas in the summer of 1951, a Jewish couple, Harry and Chaya Rachel Andres, greeted me at the train station. They spoke Yiddish to me and took me to Mrs. Haberman's home, which was in South Dallas, the largest Jewish neighborhood, where I was to stay as a boarder. I received one hundred and twenty five dollars from the Jewish Family Service for my first month. Eighty-five dollars of which was to go for my room and board. Forty dollars were for personal expenses. I did not feel comfortable getting an allowance, so that was the last time I received money from the Jewish Family Service. I landscaped the lawn of the house that Dr. Sol Haberman and his wife, Carlita, moved into. I had learned landscaping while in the Ostrowiec work camp.

After being in Dallas about a week, I went by bus to the Jewish Family Service office. On paying my bus fare, I went to an empty seat toward the back of the bus. The bus driver stopped

the bus and waved toward me. I thought he was waving to the
black people for the black people to get off the bus. He stopped
at the next stop, again motioning, and I still did not know what
was going on. He then started yelling and did not move the bus.
A man who had just gotten on the bus came in and talked to the
bus driver as he pointed to the back of the bus. The man then
came over to me and introduced himself in English. When I
shrugged my shoulders, he realized I didn't speak English. He
then asked me in Yiddish if I spoke Yiddish. I answered "Yes" in
Yiddish, and he then told me that I was not allowed to sit in the
back of the bus; the back of the bus was for the black people. He
showed me a sign on the bus saying the front was for whites and
the back was for blacks. I really couldn't understand what the
difference was, that I would have to sit in the front and the
blacks in the back of the bus. He then said, "Go to the front,
don't make any trouble," as the bus had still not moved.

I looked at him and said, "I will not go to the front; no one
can force me. I'll sit here."

He said, "Please."

I looked at him and I walked off the bus and walked to the
Jewish Family Service office. I really felt good. That was my first
experience I had in the United States.

During a meeting with the caseworker at the Jewish Family
Service, she commented that my name, Mendel Jakubowicz,
would be hard for Americans to pronounce. She asked me if I
wanted to change my name to something easier to pronounce.
She suggested Michael Jacobs, and so I took the name. Michael
because it started with an "M," and Jacobs because Jakubowicz
means "the son of Jacob."

Another experience I had soon after getting to Dallas happened at the old courthouse. It was hot and I was thirsty. I was
getting a drink of water from the water fountain, when suddenly someone grabbed me by my hair and pulled my head up. He
scared me to death. He angrily said, "You cannot drink from this
fountain."

I said, "What are you doing? Why did you grab my hair and
pull my head up?"

He said, "This fountain is for colored people, and that
fountain, over there, is for white people."

I said, "What's the difference between this water and the other water?"

People started coming over and someone said, "Don't make any trouble."

I said, "I'm not making any trouble; he's making trouble." They walked [with] me away and I left.

My first full-time job was working as a shipping clerk at a wholesale plumbing supply house. As I did not know English, I drew pictures of the items to be shipped and put them above the bins I took the parts from.

The Jewish Family Service office was in an extension of the Jewish Community Center building. Hearing of an opening in the Athletic Department, I told them in my broken English that I had taught physical fitness and that I was a gymnast. I got a part-time job. On Sundays and evenings, I taught gymnastics, physical fitness, and calisthenics. I had been in Dallas a few months. As I was just learning English, I blew my whistle to get the kids' attention and start gymnastic routines. I would then vault over the horses and show my students what to do, and they would follow me. One day, as I was teaching my gymnastics class of ten-year-olds in the gym, a girl around twenty years old walked in to the gym, stood at the side, and observed. I noticed her and said to myself, "That's my girl." I later learned her name was Ginger.

Ginger later told me that Gene Berlatsky, the center director, knowing she had a degree in physical education, after asking her to start a women's exercise program said, " You should really go down to the gym and see Mike Jacobs work with the kids. I've never seen anything like it. The gym has never been so quiet. He's a Survivor and really doesn't speak much English, but he just blows his whistle, goes hopping over the horses, and the kids follow him." Ginger and I were married October 4, 1953.

When we finally installed Swedish gym rings and a climbing rope, I also taught those skills. When the athletic director quit, I took over as interim athletic director until a new athletic director was hired.

One evening, I was driving my car on Preston Road in Dallas and about to make a right turn onto Lovers Lane. The vertical yellow lights were flashing, and I stopped to wait for the train to pass, as they do in Europe. I waited, and other drivers began to blow their horns, as they could not pass me. Finally, two policemen stopped and asked me if something was wrong with my car.

I said, "No, I'm waiting for the train to pass by."

They started laughing very hard, I can still hear them now, and then they said, "The lights are not for a train to cross—they are caution lights."

I said, "I'm sorry," and I drove on.

While working at the center, I also organized a soccer team, scheduled tournaments, and worked in the day camp. We played in the Dallas Soccer Association league. I later became president of the Dallas Soccer Association and started refereeing, as well. I also became a member of the United Stated Referees' Association. In 1967 I started refereeing professionally and retired in 1977 because of my age.

Working with the soccer programs, I divided Texas into two soccer associations, North and South Texas. We were at a soccer Association meeting in Temple, Texas. Three of us came from Dallas. There were also representatives from Houston and San Antonio. We had a discussion about the size of Texas being so large. It was a hardship for people to travel to one spot every month for our meeting. I took out a Texas map, took a pencil, and ran a line through it. I said, "that is north and that is south." That ended the discussion. I was the first president of the North Texas Soccer Association. In July of 1976 I was inducted in the North Texas Soccer Hall of Fame. I also ran clinics to teach referees. I stayed active in soccer and continued refereeing amateur games. I was honored to be a spotter [the person who identifies players and plays for the announcer] for the 1994 World Cup Games at the Dallas Cotton Bowl. It was a pleasure to work with Bill Melton, the announcer.

After working in several different jobs, I got a job with American Iron and Metals, Inc., to train as a warehouse foreman. I worked there a little over a year.

In March of 1954, I decided to open my own business, Jacobs Iron and Metal Company, Inc. I bought a one-and-a-half-ton Chevrolet stake-body truck. Being a fast learner, I soon learned to drive the truck. I would drive to the small towns and buy metals such as aluminum, copper, brass, stainless steel, and insulated copper wire. I would then grade them, separate them, and sell them to the large companies. When there were no metals to be bought, I would buy car motors or cast iron. Within several years, we had bought property and built a warehouse, and I was able to get off the road.

Through the years, the Dallas community has been good to me, and I have been involved in the both the Jewish and non-Jewish communities.

In 1956 I read that Southern Methodist University was offering an evening English course. I decided I needed to improve my English and went to enroll in the course. The course did not "make," as not enough people signed up. I then heard about the Dale Carnegie course, so I signed up, thinking that would be a good class to improve my English. When it came my time to speak, the instructor told me to back up and hold onto a table that stood in the front of the classroom. My classmates had done this as an aid to put them at ease as they introduced themselves. I looked at him and said, "I don't need to hold onto the table" and started to walk up and down as I introduced myself.

The instructor asked me if I had spoken in public before. I said, "Yes, I did."

He said, "You are in the wrong place; this is a class to teach people public speaking." He tried to return my check.

I answered, "That's okay, I signed up, and I want to stay."

For our last class we had to speak extemporaneously for five minutes. I asked the teacher what I should speak about. He said, "Something you know about." I spoke about my experiences during the Holocaust. I stopped at the end of five minutes, but the teacher and the class said, "Keep talking." I continued speaking for about an hour. After class, a couple came to me and asked that I speak to their church Sunday school class. I told them I'd be glad to speak to their class. I've been speaking ever since. I began to fulfill a promise I made myself in camp. I promised I would go and talk about the Holocaust to as many people as possible, to let them know how I lived and survived as a teenager. Since then, I have never stopped speaking and bringing the message of what one human can do to the other when we are silent and complacent—don't take it for granted, it can happen again. Groups I've spoken to since 1956 include schools, universities, community colleges, churches, synagogues, eating-disorder groups, therapists, and people at risk. I tell my audiences that I survived the torture and brutality in the ghettos and concentration camps because God gave me the strength to survive.

I survived because of three things: I never gave up hope, I never gave up my belief, and I was always positive. I tell them they are privileged to hear how I survived as a teenager. My challenge to all is not to be hateful or bitter. I tell them I do not speak with hate, and I am not bitter, either, because hate breeds hate. That is what Hitler and the Nazi machinery was all about. We must not let it happen to anyone, any place, anywhere. We must remember how beautiful it is to be free!

29

Building the Dallas Holocaust Memorial Center

1977–1984. A group of us Survivors had settled in Dallas. Some of us attended the Conservative Synagogue in Dallas. On the Day of Atonement in September 1977, during a break in the service, some of us Survivors were visiting in the open area outside the sanctuary. Included in the conversation were Frank Bell, Leon Zetley, Henry Goldberg, and Jack Stein. During our discussion, we agreed that there should be a Survivors' group, and they asked me to organize the group. I said I'd think about it. I called the first Survivors' group meeting on October 17, 1977, at my home. The group asked me to be president, and I said I would. Ginger agreed to be secretary. We decided to meet once a month and call ourselves the Holocaust Survivors in Dallas. We were a small group, but there was a feeling of camaraderie.

Our group increased with time, and although some of the members had left Germany or Poland just before the war and others had escaped to England or Russia, we had all been terrorized by the Nazis. Of course, we included the spouses, some of whom were born in the United States. Some of the second generation [children] of Holocaust Survivors were later included.

It had been a long dream of mine to have a place where we Holocaust Survivors could gather and memorialize our loved ones, as according to Jewish Tradition, the Sunday before the New Year we visit the cemetery where our family members are buried and have a memorial service. We had no cemetery to go to. As I developed my idea, I decided that we should build a memorial center for Holocaust studies, which would include a memorial room wherein we could have memorial stones on the wall.

Although we were still a somewhat small group, I decided to pursue my idea of building a Holocaust memorial center.

I had first wanted to build a freestanding building in an area in front of the Dallas Jewish Community Center. However, I could not, as the area was to become a park and would be used for the Lewis Holocaust Memorial Monument. I then wanted to use an area between the Jewish Federation of Greater Dallas and the Dallas Jewish Community Center. The area was projected to be used for a theater. Henry Cohn, who was chairman of the J.C.C. Building Committee and very supportive, suggested that I use the basement of the J.C.C., which was completely empty. We could finish it out and make it a "lower level." I decided it was better than nothing. I made a list of people to solicit money for the Holocaust center, to be paid out in five years. Some people paid me right away; it depended on how much they pledged. I went back to a small group of Holocaust Survivors, which included Leon Zetley, Sam Szor, Frank Bell, Ossie Blum, Max Glauben, David Rosenberg, and Jack Oran. I told them the story of what I had in mind. I was sitting around the table with them. They really did not want it. I guess really because they did not want to be reminded of their pain. They said, "Mike, you cannot do it. When you go to the Holocaust Survivors, they are not going to give you any money."

We talked about it, we talked about it back and forth, and they said, "Mike if you think you can do it, go ahead."

I said, "Now you are sure . . . Let me take your pledges." I soon had $75,000 from a few people. I met with Henry Cohn and his committee members, Murray Munves and Irvin Donsky, who also agreed to our using the basement space. After getting approval from the J.C.C. Board, I met with the Jewish Federation Executive Committee, who not only supported my fundraising for the Holocaust Center, but also allocated some funds. I made a list and got funds from people in other cities as well as Dallas. It did not take long for me to raise $350,000. I then called Smith and Ekblad, the architects who had enlarged the J.C.C. I went to them and said, "Look, I want to build a memorial center for Holocaust studies. I want you to design it. I've gotten permission to build it in the basement of the Jewish Community Center. Let's sit down and talk about it."

We talked about it for days and nights, and I said, "How much is it going to cost? I don't have too much money to pay the architects, you know."

Bob Ekblad said to me, "Mike, we are not going to charge you too much. We are only going to charge you for the paperwork and secretary, because this is a once-in-a-lifetime chance for us to build a center for Holocaust studies. We want to be a part of it."

Cole Smith, being a historian, was particularly interested in keeping the integrity of the Holocaust in building the center. I told them about my idea of building a boxcar as the entrance to the center. They said, "Where are you going to get the materials?

I said, "Don't worry about it. I am in the scrap business, and I'll go to the railroad company. They scrap lots of railroad boxcars, they have wood. They will be happy for me to take away the wood so they don't have to take it to the dump ground and pay for dumping it."

I couldn't sleep nights. I thought, "To build a boxcar would not have any meaning for me. I have to find a real boxcar that Jewish people were transported to ghettos and concentration camps in." We had a friend, Louis Rosenbach, who lived here in Dallas and was originally from Holland. I talked to him about the boxcar. He said he could find us a boxcar through his cousin in Holland that he could get in touch with. A few weeks later, he told me that his cousin had located a boxcar in Holland. After several months and through miscommunication, the boxcar was destroyed. After telling me that the boxcar was destroyed, he commented, "There aren't too many around." However, he said that perhaps his cousin's daughter, Jacqueline, could locate another boxcar for us.

My wife, Ginger, a sociologist, is very insistent. My friend gave me his cousin's phone number. Ginger called him and spoke to his daughter, who spoke good English. Ginger explained the situation and asked her if she would try to locate another boxcar for us. She said she would try. Within a few weeks, we spoke to her again, and she had located another box-car that was due to be destroyed in Belgium. I asked her if she could drive into Brussels to talk with the railroad commissioner, explain that the boxcar would be put in a Holocaust center, and ask that they hold the boxcar for us. She agreed to do so.

I made a special trip to Belgium and spoke with the head of the Brussels Jewish community. The man did not want to speak with me, as I had no credentials with me. He asked me who sent me and who I was. I tried to explain to him who I was and what I wanted the boxcar for, but he would not listen. I was very disappointed and flew home.

We went to a national Holocaust Survivors Gathering convention in Washington, D.C., in April of 1983. I took the mock-up model of the Holocaust Center with us to the convention display room in D.C., and while there, Ted Koppel interviewed me on "Nightline." The camera crew followed me for three days to do the interview. The television program host of "Good Morning, America" interviewed our oldest son, Mark, who was with Ginger and me. While in D.C., Ginger, in making contact with Congressmen Martin Frost and Steve Bartlett, told them about the boxcar we had located in Belgium and needed for our Holocaust center. They said we would need credentials from the State Department and were both very helpful in getting me the needed credentials for the Belgium Railroad Commission.

That June, I led a national Jewish Federation mission of professionals through Poland and went to Israel with them. When I called home from Israel, my son Andy said, "Daddy, since you are so close to Belgium, why don't you fly into Belgium and see the boxcar?" I decided that was a good idea and asked Ginger to arrange for my credentials from the State Department to be sent to the hotel where I would be staying in Brussels. My credentials were waiting for me at the hotel when I arrived on that Fourth of July. I put my suitcase in the room. I went out right quick, I took a taxi, and I went over to the Railroad Commission without calling. I went there and I said, "My name is Mike Jacobs, and I have a letter from the consulate to see you and talk about the boxcar." We talked about the boxcar and what it would be used for. He told me that the boxcar was in Antwerp. I took a taxi and drove to Antwerp. I looked at the car and walked around it. I stepped into the boxcar, and it was silent. I could see people in the boxcar and children crying. It was an overwhelming feeling. I wrote down the number of the boxcar and drove back to Brussels. They kept very good records and were able to confirm that the boxcar had been used to transport Jews to concentration camps. I told him I wanted the boxcar. The public relations man I was dealing with said, "The boxcar will cost you $850."

I took out my travelers' checks and commented, "Before I'm going to sign it, how would it look when this boxcar comes into Dallas, Texas, and I had to pay $850 for a car that transported people to their deaths? We will have news reporters, television and radio reporters, along with interviewers, wanting to know how I got the boxcar. This will be the first boxcar to be brought to the United States and all over the world of its type." He looked at me and said that he would have to go to his superiors for a decision. I left his office, and as I walked into my hotel I had a message that the car is free.

When people found out what the boxcar was going to be used for, nobody wanted to get paid for their part in shipping it to Dallas. I told them to cut off the frame and wheels of the undercarriage, as it would make for less weight, not realizing at the time that there would be no cost in shipping. I spoke to my friend Bill Betcher, at Commercial Metals, Inc., of Dallas, and asked him if he knew of a way to bring it to Dallas. I knew that his company did a lot of business with the shipping companies. He said he would look into it. He called me back and said he had a shipping company that would bring it in free of charge.

When the boxcar was unloaded in Galveston, Texas, and the Houston freight company learned what it would be used for, they did not charge to bring the car to Dallas. It was very exciting seeing a brand-new rig bring the boxcar onto the parking lot of the Jewish Community Center, where I climbed up on top of the car, checked the cables, and hooked the chains before the crane unloaded the boxcar and set it on the parking lot. After the boxcar was placed on the parking lot, people came from all over to see it. Someone left a pot of white chrysanthemums in the middle of the boxcar. We were so touched to see the flowers. The news, television, and radio reporters also came to write the story. I was interviewed by news media wanting to know how the car got to Dallas, Texas.

When I was sitting with the architects day and night, we were talking about the memorial center, and as I was talking to them, they were designing it. I said I want the Memorial Room completely different. I want a gate at the front of the room that we can open and close. They said it would be no problem. They said the gate would have bars on it. When they looked at my face, they said, "Mike, you don't like it, do you?"

I said, "I don't. Five and a half years being in the ghettos and the concentration camps . . . I don't want to look out again."

I told them the story about the city of mine, how the books and scrolls were taken out of the synagogue and the attached house of study to the square near the synagogue and put on fire. "That's how I want it to look. I want a gate that you can open and close. When you look at the bottom of the gate, I want people to imagine different sizes of prayer books burning. When the gate is closed you will be able to see a scroll that is also being inflamed. It will look like everything is going up in flames. I will call it the 'Gate of Fire.' As you walk past the gate, there will be a bronze everlasting light designed by Ruth Litwin hanging from the ceiling. The light will look like a flame. On the walls there will be memorial stones put up for the people who died in the ghettos and concentration camps. On one of the walls there will be stones put up in memory of individual members of the family that died in the Holocaust by surviving members of the Holocaust and other relatives. The next wall will have only stones for families. Another wall will have memorial stones with names of the Righteous Gentiles who endangered their own and their families' lives to save Jewish people. The wall at the back of the room will always remain empty, to show the void, to remember the millions of people who were murdered. The walls will be white because white represents hope. There will be a large memorial stone surrounded by pillars with the inscriptions of different concentration camps chained around with make-believe electrified barbed wire. There will be an inscription, written not with hate, but with love, on the large memorial stone. There will be a bronze sculpture that Ruth Litwin will sculpt, representing people burning, with a hand reaching out (which I later named "Grasping for Life"). Six lights representing the six million Jews murdered in the Holocaust will be between the sculpture and the large memorial stone. There will be a bronze urn beneath the sculpture shaped like a Star of David, filled with remains of human bones that I brought back from Auschwitz II, Birkenau, to be laid to rest. People will stand here in the biggest cemetery ever known to mankind. The audio-visual room will display pictures and artifacts of the Holocaust. There will also be a screen on which to show video. The other room will house a library, and there will be offices.

"This Holocaust center will be built with love, and not with hate. It is being built for future generations as a reminder of what one human can do to another if we are silent and complacent. We must remember and never forget."

By the time we dedicated the Dallas Memorial Center for Holocaust Studies, the Survivors appreciated what I had done. The wanted to name the Memorial Room in my honor. I thanked them and told them I appreciated the gesture, but the Memorial Room is dedicated to the six million of our brothers, sisters, mothers, fathers, and extended family who perished in the enormous tragedy, the Holocaust. No one should rob those souls of a memorial dedicated solely to them. That room is sacred to their memory and must remain so.

We dedicated the Memorial Room of the Holocaust Center on January 29, 1984, with a special ceremony honoring the memory of six million Jews, including over a million children. I spoke about the symbolism, and members of the Survivors group, followed by audience members from all walks of life, put the bone fragments I had brought from Auschwitz II-Birkenau into the bronze urn.

The Dallas Memorial Center for Holocaust Studies opened officially with a special program on April 15, 1984. Dignitaries present included U.S. Congressman Martin Frost, Texas Governor Mark White and his wife, and Arlington Mayor Tommy Vandergriff, along with many heads of local Jewish agencies. The auditorium at the Jewish Community Center was filled. To found the Dallas Memorial Center for Holocaust Studies made my dream come true.

EPILOGUE

Konin was a city with a population of about 12,000 people. Before the war, there was a nice Jewish community in Konin, with about 3,500 [over 3,000] Jews. Most of the Jews were merchants with little stores—tailors, shoemakers, and other professions. We had two Jewish doctors and some Jewish dentists and lawyers in the city. The Jewish people were very, very involved in the daily life of the community. I had a big family from my mother's side in the city, and my father's side lived in some of the surrounding cities.

Before the war, there were 3.5 million Jews in Poland. When I first visited Poland after the war in 1975, I was told that fewer than 6,000 Jews still lived in Poland. Some survivors immigrated to different countries between the years of 1945 and 1975, but the enormous tragedy of the war years was evident.

During this Holocaust, six million Jews were killed, including about one and a half million children. About five million non-Jews, including almost half a million Gypsies, died. I lost my three brothers, my father, my mother, and my two sisters. I am the only survivor in my family. I lost close to eighty of my relatives that I remember and am sure other family members were lost. My family and relatives died in Treblinka, a camp of no return. One brother died as a Jewish freedom fighter.

Today, I do not even have photos of all my family members. I wrote to the forest ranger after the war, hoping I could get back the pictures of my family I had hidden in his little barn. He wrote back saying, no, he didn't still have the family pictures. The bad weather had destroyed them.

I was never a teenager. I spent all my teenage years in the concentration camps. I lived on less than 800 calories a day of food, working twelve-hour days, every day. I was tortured; I was beaten. I've got scars on my face, but I always stood up. I always bounced back and said to myself, "Someday, I'm going to be free."

I was one of the lucky ones. I survived. I had a chance for a new life—to get married and raise my wonderful children, to see my granddaughters growing up. I am a living survivor from the atrocities and the genocide. I want all young people to know what one human can do to the other. It can happen again. Never take your freedom for granted. I know how beautiful it is to be free.

Hate breeds hate. But we cannot, we must not, be silent or complacent. If we are, this can happen again. That's what I want people to know. It makes no difference what kind of circumstances you are in, how bad they are, the ups and downs; you can always bounce back. Always tell yourself, "Tomorrow's going to be a nicer day. I will do it." Think positively. That's what I believed in then, and I still believe in it. It's a better future. Don't let yourself down. Always tell yourself, "No, I'm not going to let myself down." That's what I did.

APPENDIX 1

Timeline
of Mike Jacobs' Holocaust Experience

1939
- German invasion of Poland (September 1)
- Invasion of Konin, Poland, Mike Jacobs' hometown
- Jews of Konin sent to the city of Ostrowiec (November)
- Ghetto established in Ostrowiec. Mike and his family live in cramped quarters with two other families (a total of sixteen people in a small room divided into three sections)

1942
- Liquidation of the large ghetto in Ostrowiec (summer)
- Smaller ghetto created in Ostrowiec
- Mike Jacobs' family (minus Mike and his brother Reuven) is sent to death camp at Treblinka
- After a short stay in the smaller ghetto, Reuven escapes to fight with the Jewish partisans

1943
- Reuven killed while fighting with the partisans for the liberation of Poland (February)
- Liquidation of the smaller ghetto in Ostrowiec. Remaining Jews are sent to a labor camp in Ostrowiec

1944
- Mike Jacobs sent to Auschwitz-Birkenau (June). Most of his internment will be spent in Birkenau

1945

- Mike Jacobs is one of the 60,000 prisoners sent on a death march from Auschwitz-Birkenau (January 18). The march covers thirty-five kilometers (13 miles) a day, over a period of five days, in the snow; many die of starvation, while others are shot. Only about 24,000 survive the Death March
- Death March survivors forced into gondola railcars at a junction
- Mike Jacobs taken to Mauthausen/Gusen II
- Working as a machinist in Gusen II, Mike Jacobs (at great personal risk) able to sabotage German planes
- Mike Jacobs' camp liberated by the Thunderbolts, the 11th Armored Division of the U.S. Army (May 5)
- Unwilling to be placed in a Displaced Persons' Camp, Mike Jacobs walks into Linz

• • •

After five and a half years of ghettos and camps, Mike Jacobs, at the age of nineteen years, six months, weighed only seventy pounds.
The youngest of six children, Mike lost his entire immediate family and over eighty members of his extended family in the Holocaust.

• • •

Post-War

- Mike remains in Mittenwald, Germany, for five and a half years, teaching athletics, organizing sports groups, and working as a shopkeeper (during this time, Mike went back to school and graduated from The Seminar for Sports Instructors in 1946)
- In 1951 Mike moves to Dallas, Texas, with the assistance of the Jewish Joint Distribution Committee and HIAS (Hebrew Immigrant Aid Society)
- After settling in Dallas, Mike Jacobs becomes involved in many organizations within the Jewish community. He is a major force in the development of a Dallas soccer program
- In 1953 Mike marries a native Dallasite, Ginger Chesnick. They have four children: Mark, Debbie J. Linksman, Andy, and Reuben, and four grandchildren, Rivka, Leeza, Sarah, and Aviva
- Mike starts Jacobs Iron and Metal Company in 1954 and becomes a leader in the scrap industry. The company evolves into The Jacobs Group
- In 1977 Mike organizes the Holocaust Survivors in the Dallas area (later disbanded after the opening of the Memorial Center)
- Mike Jacobs founds the Dallas Memorial Center for Holocaust Studies, which opens April 15, 1984

APPENDIX 2

Maps

CENTRAL EUROPE, 1929

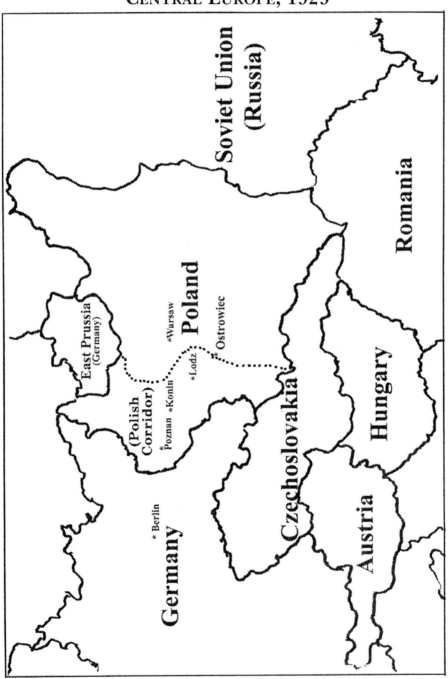

190

POLAND, PRESENT-DAY

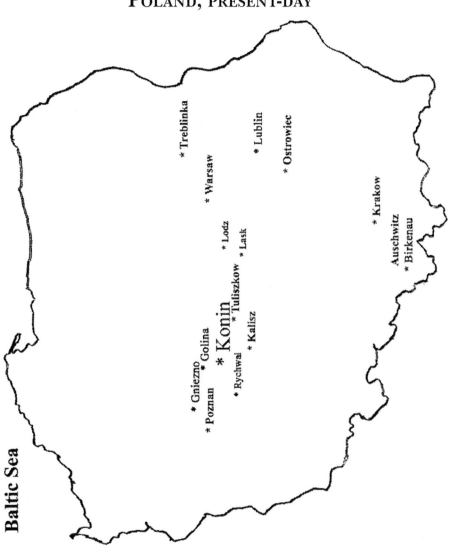

* Treblinka

* Warsaw

* Lublin

* Ostrowiec

* Krakow

* Lodz

* Lask

Auschwitz
* Birkenau

Konin

* Tuliszkow

* Kalisz

* Gniezno
* Golina

* Poznan

* Rychwal

Baltic Sea

KONIN

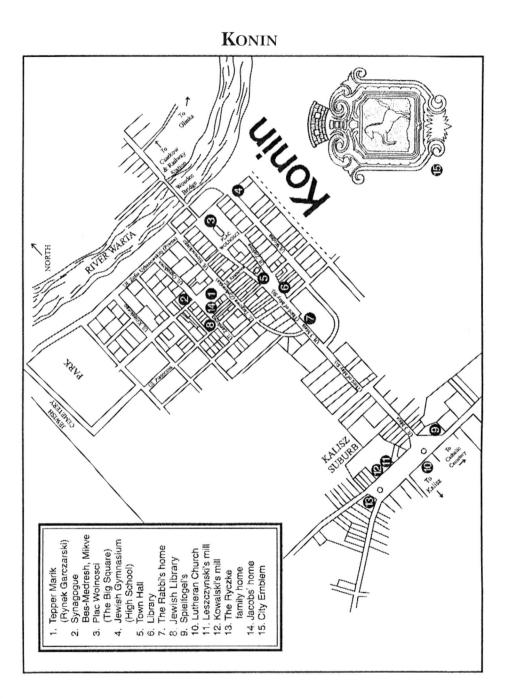

1. Tepper Marik
   (Rynek Garczarski)
2. Synagogue
   Bes-Medresh, Mikve
3. Plac Wolnosci
   (The Big Square)
4. Jewish Gymnasium
   (High School)
5. Town Hall
6. Library
7. The Rabbi's home
8. Jewish Library
9. Spielfogel's
10. Lutheran Church
11. Leszczynski's mill
12. Kowalski's mill
13. The Ryczke
    family home
14. Jacobs' home
15. City Emblem

GERMANY, 1942

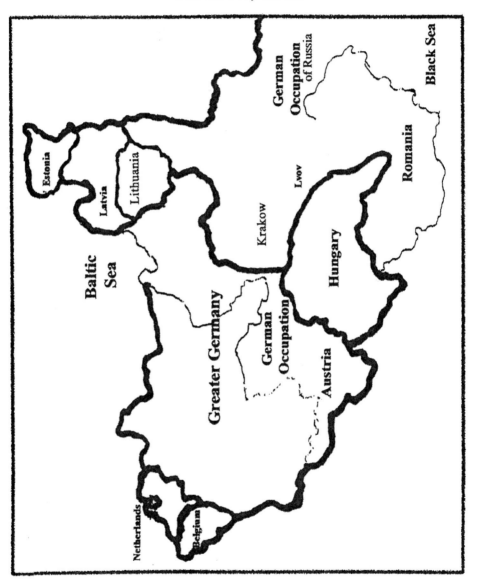

APPENDIX 3

Correspondence and Articles

Mike Jacobs has spoken publicly about the Holocaust since 1956. By now, he has spoken to and estimated 500,000 people! Mike's collection of letters and articles fills fifty-two three-inch binders. His collection grows constantly as he continues speaking.

This small sampling of letters, newspaper articles, and student writings illustrates the effect he has on his audience. Some names have been omitted for the sake of privacy.

• • •

Lakeview Centennial High School
Garland, Texas
February 26, 1992

Mr. Jacobs,

Sir, I would first like to tell you that I am in no way being forced to write a letter to you. No, I am writing you because, and only because, I wanted to. I wanted to write to you and express to you my feelings on the Holocaust. To me, life is so precious. Now, I too have scars on my arms, not because someone else put them there, but because at one time in my short life, I tried to end my life. I had attempted this in many ways, one of which left some pretty big scars. I have also been through a time when I had a swastika carved into my arm, which is still very visible today.

I believe in what you have told me, that hate surely breeds hate. And I think that I have found that out the hard way. Now I realize just how precious my life is. Sure, there are still some days when I wish I were dead, but I realize that I, too, must live. You realized why you had to live, to tell your story and help the world refrain from repeating history. But I have realized that I must live for a different reason, and I'm not sure what that is yet, but I will stick around to find out. You may now be wondering why I am telling you this, but my reason is that you made me realize that whatever my problem is and how big it may seem, it's never so big that I cannot handle it.

I do not believe in hate. I can honestly say that I do not hate anyone. I also do not believe in being mean or cruel to another human being. I just can't do it, and I won't. It's funny, because when I used to think Nazis were cool and believed in swastikas, I never realized what I actually believed in. I only thought that they had to do with Blacks and Whites, but I was so wrong. I know that now, and I don't believe in those things now. I don't think I ever truly believed in them . . . .

Sir, I just wanted to tell you that I truly feel that it takes a very special person to devote as much time to something as you do. I am so happy to know that our generation has someone like yourself to inform us firsthand. I am truly sorry that my children will not be so lucky. Thank you, sir, for coming to our school and speaking to us. Whether you know ir or not, you have changed so many people's lives, including mine.

—A. O.

• • •

8-11-92

Dear Mr. Mike Jacobs,

I came yesterday with my group home, the Benavides. I am a former skinhead. I was on drugs for 3½ years, since I was about 12 years old. I am 15 years old now and have been clean and sober for almost 8 months. My interest with the skinheads grew as I got into more drugs. As you said, I did not believe that the Holocaust really happened. So when I came to the presentation yesterday, I was determined to ignore what you said. But as you were talking, I started to think very hard about my old beliefs, and I said to myself, how could anyone make up such a big lie and keep that lie alive for so many years, and if Hitler was really humane, then how could all those people die so quickly and so brutally?

You've made such an impact in my life that just thanking you won't do. When I tried to commit suicide, I felt that all my problems were huge, and they could only be fixed by death, but when you spoke about your life and the trauma that you went through, I could only say my problems were nothing compared to [that]. I also feel that if you survived that terrible life, then I certainly can survive mine. I admire what you've accomplished in your life—speaking about your past and touching so many people is tremendous. If someday everyone was like you, this world would be a better place.

> Thank you,
> J. W.

•   •   •

April 17, 1991

Dear Mr. Mike Jacobs—
    Yesterday I was fortunate to have the opportunity to visit
your center and hear you speak of your experiences, along with
a few other SMU students enrolled in Professor Tyson's class.
Wishing to express my gratitude to you but not finding the
words at the memorial center, I have decided instead to write
you a note. [Hearing] you speak of your experiences from a first-
person perspective, I think for all of us it was finally an opportunity to place an actual face on all of the data and [discover] a
reality beyond the old newsreels and books that . . . my generation (unfortunately) tends to distance [itself] from.
    I have been. . . informed about the Holocaust for much of
my life [and]. . . have had to struggle with the questions that it
brings up. My great uncle was among the liberators at one of the
camps, and he openly shared his story with me. It is only now
that I realize why. Now a student at the University studying
German and German culture, I have become more and more
disturbed by this knowledge of the Holocaust and frankly was
not sure what to do with it. Having spent time in Germany, perhaps I was. . . looking for an answer. How could these people
commit such a crime? These people who were so nice to me,
with smiling faces and kind words, how could they do such a
thing? Regardless of the fact that neither myself nor my family
is of Jewish descent, to me it is a human issue. So, I write all of
these words to express to you the wonderful feeling I had when
you spoke only of love and not of hate. You do not hate the
Germans for what has happened—and neither shall I. It may
sound silly, but perhaps I needed your "seal of approval" to for-
give the Germans as a whole for what has happened.
    This is not to say that I wish to forget—and you have my hon-
est promise that I will for the rest of my life defend the fact that the
Holocaust did occur and pass this knowledge on to the next generation. It won't be forgotten. And if I should ever have children,
they will hear the story and of the time that I was able to meet an
actual survivor—so that they, too, will not doubt its existence.
    I would like to conclude this letter by thanking you for your
words of hope and strength. Witnessing myself that you were

able to survive such trials and [that you are] now able to laugh, be happy and hopeful, and to love, is truly an inspiration. I know whatever obstacles I encounter in my life can be overcome—and I will keep you in mind for reassurance. Although I must admit I'm not terribly religious, I would like to say, God bless you and your work, both now and in the future.

Best wishes, and many thanks again,
K. D.
SMU Class of 1998

• • •

November 29, 1999
By Wendy Topletz
[Essay explaining who her hero is, and why]

After his inspirational story of the Holocaust, I guess it could be told that Mike Jacobs is my hero. By surviving the horrible darkness of World War II, he is a very courageous man, strong in his faith. As a true believer of Judaism, he never once gave up hope in God, even through his worst struggles. Mike Jacobs is a brilliant man who made the Holocaust a moment to remember forever. Despite the awful experiences he has been through, his positive attitude has brought him much success. Though the Nazis stripped Mr. Jacobs of his name, his family, and his friends, he never surrendered his soul. His faith and optimistic outlook on life are what I admire about him. Mr. Jacobs is a nice and generous man, and he has donated so much to the Jewish community. This, in Yiddish, is what we call a *mensch*. Mr. Jacobs has done so much more than survive the Holocaust—he spends his life making others aware of it.

He is actually quite close to my family, and my grandfather, Jules Colton, who landed Mr. Jacobs his first job when he came to Dallas.

Mike Jacobs brought soccer to North Texas, and most importantly, made so many people aware of the Holocaust. This man is my hero.

• • •

February 16, 2000

Dear Mr. Jacobs:

Mere words cannot describe my appreciation to you for your time and presentation to the Richardson High School Theater students last Thursday. Although it must be painful for you to describe the horrors that you endured, I can tell you that the impact it made with these high school students made all the difference in the world.

I wish you could have been there later in the day when we gathered them all together to process what they learned and discuss how it could be applied to the play and the characters they portray. I don't think any of them had really understood the degree of horror that the Nazis created in the Shoah. They all were enlightened, and the raw emotions expressed were incredible. Your story touched them to the core, and none of them will look at life the same way again. Many expressed the feeling that they would think before making a comment about someone's race or religion again, because they saw what "doing nothing" can do. Since that day, their rehearsals have been intense. Before they were just playacting, but now it is real to them.

The most prevalent message that came across and touched them was your belief in never giving up hope. We all have moments in our lives when all seems hopeless, but your description of endurance and faith made us realize that hope is what will keep us going. Thank you for sharing that gift.

Once again, from the bottom of my heart, thank you. I watched a miracle evolve last Thursday, in the transformation of attitudes and perceptions. Only your willingness to share made that possible.

Sincerely yours,
Sally Grant Finberg

• • •

[From Joan Weston's Brookhaven College class]
Journal 14
February 26th–29th

Well, today we went to the Holocaust museum. It was an unbelieveable experience, you know. I know so much about the concentration camps and the whole history, and I knew it would be a somber experience, and that knowing myself I would get upset and possibly shed a few tears. But I was astounded at my reaction. I've seen Spielberg's movie and have actually met survivors before, but I knew that they were because I saw their numbers. We never spoke about the experience; we only exchanged pleasantries, and I pretended I hadn't noticed. Not because I meant them any disrespect, but because I thought it would have been obnoxious and cruel to mention the things running through my mind. I've always thought it would inflict needless pain on them, and I didn't want to do that.

So today when I met Mike, I was overwhelmed with emotion. During his lecture, I was already upset, because it was so apparent that he really was reliving the memories. I could feel his pain, but only, of course, [to a much lesser degree]. I felt overwhelmed by the inhumanity of man. Hurt by the confusion, not physically, but deep down in the core of my existence, in the most innocent and private place of all that I am. When he spoke of the baby he held in his arms, and of how he could still feel the warmth of the child, my heart swelled with pain for him. He has to carry that with him every moment of every day of his life. He is so courageous. Not because he survived, but because he must live each day of the rest of his life for all of the people who were lost. Every one of those people lives in the soul of Mike Jacobs. You can see them looking out through his eyes when he beseeches you never to forget, to never fall silent. They walk every step with him, supporting him when he tires.

How can he live with the pain and still love humanity?. . .

After the lecture, Mike walked out with me and a friend and was speaking to me about the horror of Pat Buchanan running for president, how [Buchanan] believed there was not a Holocaust. I wanted so desperately to make some kind of connection with him, some brief, fleeting bond that would be

ingrained in my memory. But I couldn't even speak. I was totally overcome with emotions. Tears were silently running down my
face, and he looked into my eyes, and I saw that he thought me
so young and foolish. As if he was almost taken aback by my dis-
tress, he looked genuinely surprised. All I could say was, "Mike,"
and then I was practically hyperventilating from trying to hold
back my crying.

He touched my arm and said, "You feel things deeply, you
have many feelings."

I then started sobbing, almost as if he had given me permission. I was still very embarrassed. I felt so foolish. Here was
this kind man who had given us a beautiful gift. He had exposed
his innermost, painful memories to us, he had shared himself
selflessly so that we might never feel the horrors and pain he
had. And what do I do? I blubber all over him!!

We then entered the museum through the [railroad] cart. I
was leaning against the wall thinking it was a replica, and then
he told us it had actually transported people. I wondered if the
wood I had leaned against had supported someone just like me,
with the same hopes and dreams. Had they leaned their head
against those same wood fibers? I just couldn't bear the emotions. It really was awful.

We then toured the museum, and I really do wish I could
have been alone with my thoughts. Then Mike came over and
pointed out the bones he had brought back from the last trip.
He kept asking if I saw the bones. They seemed to hold a special significance for him, like a special representation for the
whole experience. But the most disturbing items for me were the
ones Mike carried in his big black bag. When he held up the bar
of soap and explained what it was made of, I nearly became ill.
I didn't want to deal with how it made me feel. When he showed
us his cap. . . well, it really drove everything home, it was so sym-
bolic. The way he held it in his hands was different than the
other items. He held it with such reverence. As if it was the most
treasured item he owned. It broke my heart. But when he lifted
out the baby shoes, I really wanted to flee. I really wanted so
much to get up and walk out of that room—to walk away from
the pain. Because I could—but I didn't, because it symbolized to
me the fact that Mike never had that option. No matter how

atrocious the evils were, he couldn't remove himself from the situation. In his mind he could, or in his soul he could fly away, but he always had to come back to the nightmare. So there was no way I was going to walk out on Mike. No way.

Afterward, at the end of the tour, I came over to you all because I wanted to speak to him. He was talking about Buchanan again. I think he really couldn't believe that someone who was running for president and who was doing surprisingly well truly thought that the Holocaust was a farce. It seems to me that even after everything he's been through and all the different kinds of people he has spoken to, this was still very hard for him to comprehend, to have to believe, to have to accept. I just listened to the conversation, but didn't really trust that if I tried to speak I wouldn't start crying again. . . .

[Later] I walked over to thank Mike for the morning. I thought, Here is your last chance, don't blow it. Well, what do you think happened? Now, you don't know me very well, but I'm sure it's not hard to imagine. All I got out was, "Thank you so much, Mike," and started welling up again. He was very gracious. He took my hand in both of his and asked me my name. I told him . . . and he told me to come back again and to please bring someone with me. Then I stumbled away, trying not to start sobbing again . . . .

All I can say is that I am truly thankful for the opportunity to have gone this morning. . . . I think . . . that [I] somehow, somewhere lost the path I had truly wanted to travel. I have made excuses . . . in my mind: "I have this working against me," "I'm too old now," "It won't happen." After today, meeting Mike, hearing his story, I have a newfound perspective. I realize that I can do whatever I put my mind to. I am capable of anything and everything. My hopes and dreams are burning brighter than they have in a long time. They had burned low and weakened, my flames have not warmed my soul for a while. But I realize I just lost my way . . . . I feel invincible. I am all, and everything is me. I am one but joined to all, and therefore I can and will make a difference. Mike Jacobs gave me a beautiful gift when he shared his life's experiences, but he saved my soul when he inspired me. I only wish I could give him a gift as special in return.

• • •

The Dallas Morning News
Tuesday, October 11, 1994
"Congratulations"
[Letter to the Editor]

I just read your story about Michael Jacobs receiving the Hope for Humanity award. I just want to say "congratulations."

Mr. Jacobs came to my ninth-grade world history class and told his story in 1979 at Richardson Junior High School. He made such an impression on me that to this day I think about him and remember his story. I have also visited the Dallas Memorial Center for Holocaust Studies and have found it to be very informative. It has built on the knowledge he gave me when I was in school. He has done a great job!

I will never forget Mr. Jacobs or the story he told of the victims and the survivors of the Holocaust. I will pass their story on to my daughter and my grandchildren, because, as Mr. Jacobs told our class back in 1979, we must never forget. If we do, it can happen again.

Thank you, Mr. Jacobs, for all you do. Keep educating people, and if we all do our part, we can make sure the Holocaust or anything like it will never happen again.

Jamie Specht
Plano

• • •

November 8, 1994

Dear Mr. Jacobs,

I really enjoyed seeing you again when I brought my daughter Amanda to see you. After my Camp Fire meeting on Sunday, I decided to do something that I have been wanting to do for a long time. I decided to see if I could transfer the tape that I have of our interview back in 1980 when I was a junior at Berkner to a small microcassette. This would enable me to use it in my transcribing machine (it's my new "toy," and I love it).

I have been concerned that the large tape might get damaged from listening to it so much. . . I was successful in getting the interview transferred to the small tape, so I have transcribed your interview.

I have to tell you that even though I have listened to our interview many times, typing it was a completely different experience. As I typed, I found myself completely absorbed. I was actually there with you, and in my mind's eye, I could see exactly what you were saying.

The reason that I have transcribed your interview is twofold. The first is to preserve it in written form for myself, should anything ever happen to my tape, and the second is to give it to you. I have typed it exactly as you spoke on the tape (although there are some words that were German and I did not know how to spell them), and I want you to have it just in case you decide to write your book or to simply put it in the library there at the center.

When you decide to write your book, I would like to offer to you, as a volunteer, my eyes, ears, and fingers to do the transcribing. All you would have to do is tell what you want to be typed into a microcassette recorder . . . Take care of yourself and your family, and please let me know if I can help you.

Sincerely,
Jamie Specht

P.S. If you want to tell [your story] to someone while taping [it], just give me a call. I'm all ears.

• • •

April 14, 1983

Mr. Mike Jacobs
Jacobs Iron & Metal

Dear Mike:

I want you to know that your friends who were born after the war and in this country were very proud to see you on "Nightline" as the outstanding spokesman you were for the remembrance of the Holocaust.

I am very proud to have known you all these years, and I am very pleased to have the opportunity, in my way, to work for these causes. I promise you that I will keep up the work that I do to never let people forget what happened to our people during the Holocaust.

Sincerely yours,
Phillip A. Aronoff

• • •

United Press International
Oct. 11, 1983

Dear Mark,

This story on your father's project got some well-deserved attention from UPI's general desk in Washington.

It played out today on our A-wire, the one reserved for major stories of worldwide significance.

Hope you are doing well.
Yours,
Debbie Wormser

[Attatched to Ms. Wormser's letter is a printout of the AP wire story, below.]

Nazi Railroad Boxcar Becomes Monument and Reminder

Dallas (UPI)—A railroad boxcar, its paint faded and its ironwork rusted, sits on wooden blocks in front of the Jewish Community Center of North Dallas, a reminder of a black era in world history.

Mike Jacobs, who coordinated a volunteer effort to have the boxcar shipped from Belgium to North Texas, during an interview said it is a reminder of horror for thousands of people such as himself who survived the Nazi Holocaust.

"When Americans are told about boxcars they think of them as big and huge. This boxcar was built to hold 12 cows," Jacobs said of the vehicle, which is about 35 feet long, 10 feet wide and 10 feet high.

"The one I was packed into along with my family and about 100 others was about this size. I was in one corner of the car, my mother in another and the rest of the family somewhere else.

"I could hear them screaming. Every time I enter this car, I can hear my mother and sisters screaming. I never saw them again. You see, I can still smell and see the tears, blood, corpses in this car."

The boxcar, identified by the faded letter "B" on its side as belonging to the national railroad of Belgium, was one of thousands used by Nazis to transport Jews from throughout Europe to concentration camps.

Jacobs said he, his parents, three brothers and two sisters were herded into one such boxcar in 1939 and taken to Treblinka, where his entire family was put to death. Jacobs, 14 at the time, was shuttled from one camp to another for five years.

He was rescued by U.S. troops on May 5, 1945, from the Mauthausen camp in Austria and brought to Dallas when he was 19. Jacobs now runs an iron scrap business. He and his wife of 35 years have three sons and a daughter.

The boxcar was donated by the government of Belgium to the Dallas Jewish Organization. Workmen are setting up the display this month, and soon it will become part of the Holocaust studies center Jacobs is establishing.

"I want this to be a constant reminder of what the Nazis did to us," he said.

Jacobs, who still has his inmate number B-4990 tatooed on his left forearm, said the boxcar brings back horrible memories to many people. Some refuse to step inside.

That, Jacobs said, is the point.

"We need to keep telling the world again nd again that this is what happened and it can happen again," he said.

Jacobs said he has no bitterness in him and wouldn't take revenge on those who killed his family if they were brought before him today.

"I have a very wonderful family and I have learned what it is to love and be loved," he said.

UPI 10-11-83

• • •

Longview News-Journal
Saturday, January 6, 1996
"Remember . . . never forget"
By Jill Hathaway

Mike Jacobs survived some of the ugliest atrocities ever committed, but his story speaks of something glorious within the human spirit.

The 70-year-old Holocaust survivor said time and again during a visit to St. Mary Catholic School on Friday that it was "hope and belief and thinking positive" that kept him going during five and a half years in Jewish ghettos and Nazi concentration camps.

Jacobs, who is founder of the Dallas Memorial Center for Holocaust Studies, spent more than two hours with Nancy Walker's eighth-grade language-arts class.

The students also heard from Walker's father, Brown Nelson, who was among the American forces that liberated the Dachau concentration camp in Germany.

Nelson cautioned the youth not to believe those who contend the Holocaust never happened. "I'm here to tell you it did happen like Mr. Jacobs said."

Jacobs, born Mendel Jakubowicz in Poland, was robbed of his youth, his family and nearly his life.

He was 14 years old when the German army invaded Poland in 1939. The 19-year-old Jacobs weighed 70 pounds when he was liberated by American soldiers from a camp in Austria on May 5, 1945.

"Ladies and gentlemen, you are privileged to listen to a Holocaust survivor," Jacobs said to the St. Mary students, adding that their children and grandchildren will not have that opportunity. "Ten to 15 years from now, no Holocaust survivors will be around to tell the story. It's up to you.

"If you walk out of here hateful and bitter, I have accomplished nothing," Jacobs said. "Remember what one human being can do to another.

"It can happen again if we are silent and complacent," he warned. "You must remember how beautiful it is to be free."

Jacobs, who began telling his story in 1956, believes the reason he lived was to tell what happened. "I feel good when people want to listen to me," he said. "I get so much energy and strength from it."

The Dallas resident, who immigrated to the United States in 1951, has led tours of former concentration camp sites in Europe.

In 1986, Jacobs made a very personal pilgrimage with his family to Treblinka, Poland, and the site of a German concentration camp where his mother, father, three brothers and two sisters were killed. There he wept uncontrollably at a stone memorial erected by the Polish government.

As a teen-ager he had endured hard labor, torture, constant guessing about who would be "selected" for the gas chamber and a 'death march" as Russian forces closed in.

Jacobs showed the students the prisoner number that was tatooed on his arm and the scar he sustained on his forehead from a beating with a bullwhip.

He was imprisoned in the Ostrowicz and Auschwitz-Birkenau concentration camps in Poland, as well as Mauthausen and Gusen II in Austria.

Between 10,000 and 15,000 people died [daily] in the gas chambers at Auschwitz-Birkenau. Children were thrown alive into pits while German SS troops laughed.

As German armies advanced throughout Europe, Jews often fled to or were driven into areas of cities where they were forced to live in appalling conditions.

Jacobs recalled how he was forced, under command of an SS sergeant, to clear houses in one such Jewish ghetto of belongings left behind by families forced into concentration camps. Some desperate parents left behind their own children, hoping they would be rescued.

In one home, Jacobs found a baby screaming in a crib, he said.

"I can still feel the warmth of that child," whom he picked up. But he was forced to take the baby to a tall building. He had to watch, in horror, as children were thrown from the windows. SS troops also shot into the windows of that building and argued about who had the best aim.

Speaking to the St. Mary students, Jacobs held up a 50-year-old pair of children's shoes, which had been carefully tied together by one of the millions of mothers put to death.

These shoes, he said, "represent over 1 million children. Remember . . . never forget."

●   ●   ●

From *Dateline World Jewry,* April 2002

INVESTIGATION

A Polish government institute has begun investigating the decades-old allegations that a Nazi-run anatomy institute in the city of Gdansk experimented with making soap from human remains.

A detailed report by a Polish Soviet-era commission in 1946 indicated that in 1944, about 90 pounds of soap were made from human remains under the supervision of Rudolph Spanner, a German professor who ran the institute during World War II.

Dallas Morning News
6-19-98
Holocaust survivor teaches tolerance
Dallas man lost 80 relatives in Nazi death camps
By Sandy Louey

Mike Jacobs never wants to forget the Holocaust.

The 72-year-old Dallas resident survived more than five years in ghettos and Nazi concentration camps. More than 80 members of his family, including his parents and five siblings, died.

For more than 40 years, he has dedicated his life to educating others about the genocide that claimed the lives of 6 million European Jews during World War II. High schools, churches, civic groups, universities—he speaks at them all.

Mr. Jacobs, who founded the Dallas Memorial Center for Holocaust Studies, said he wants his listeners not to take freedom for granted and to speak up when they see bigotry and prejudice.

"I do not speak with hate," he said. "I want you to remember what one person can do to another if you're silent and complacent."

On Wednesday night, his audience at the North Branch of the Jewish Community Center in Plano numbered just six. But the size of the crowd is not what matters, he said. It's that others hear his stories.

"We must remember and never forget," said Mr. Jacobs, who said there are about 100 Holocaust survivors in the Dallas area.

Neal Abramson of Richardson, who attended Wednesday's talk, said he finds it incredible that some still deny that the Holocaust happened, especially with the accounts of survivors such as Mr. Jacobs.

"He stands as the evidence that it cannot be denied," he said.

Mr. Jacobs grew up as the youngest of six children in Konin, Poland. In 1939, his family was herded with others to the town square and into boxcars, where they traveled for three days without food or water.

They ended up in a ghetto in Ostrowiec, where 16 people were crammed together in a small room.

In 1942, he was separated from his family, which was sent to Treblinka, a concentration camp. A brother who had joined the underground resistance was killed.

Mr. Jacobs remained in Ostrowiec, where he worked for an SS officer who searched for valuables in the apartments of Jews who had been deported.

He says he saw SS troops tossing babies from windows to use as target practice. An old man was shot to death in his arms.

"That's what humans can do to one another," he said.

In 1944, he was sent to Auschwitz-Birkenau, where he thought the smoke coming from the chimneys was from baking bread. When he got closer, he realized the smell was not of bread, but of human skin.

Hot water flowed in the shower house where he was sent, but others were gassed to death in such places.

Those people never had a chance," he said.

From Auschwitz, he was taken on a death march in the snow to Mauthausen-Gusen II in Austria. He stayed there until American troops liberated him on May 5, 1945.

He was 19 and weight 70 pounds.

"They can torture my body, but they can't torture my spirit," he said.

Mr. Jacobs said he believes he survived because he was able to dream and fantasize even though he never knew if he would make it to the next day.

"I never gave up my hope," said Mr. Jacobs, who moved to Dallas in 1951. "I always believed that I was going to survive."

Audience member Kim Finkelman of Dallas, who starts as a teacher at Bowman Middle School in Plano this fall, said prejudice and bigotry occur every day around the world.

People should not stand quietly by while others are being persecuted, she said.

"If they don't stand up and say something, that's when problems can begin," she said.

• • •

An issue that has been debated in the area of Holocaust history is whether the Nazis made soap from their victims' corpses. The following article and refutation appeared in the Dallas Morning News.

Dallas Morning News
Tuesday, September 26, 2000
Holocaust Museum Disputes Book's Soap Account
Associated Press

Atlanta—The U.S. Holocaust Museum has barred a book signing by the nephew of an Auschwitz inmate who suggests Nazis made soap out of the bodies of Jews who died in concentration camps.

In a memoir published this spring, Ben Hirsch wrote that while at Auschwitz, his uncle was forced to make soap and that human corpses were used as a raw material.

Mr. Hirsch, whose parents and two siblings died in the campos, also was among a group of people who buried four bars of soap at an Atlanta cemetery's Holocaust memorial in 1970, believing the soap to be made of human fat.

But many historians say the Nazis never used their victims to make soap, and the United States Holocaust Memorial Museum refuses to endorse any book that argues otherwise.

Mr. Hirsch, an Atlanta architect, had planned a signing of his book *Hearing a Different Drummer* at the Washington museum in November, but museum officials said allowing him to do so would be interpreted as sanctioning his views, *The Atlanta Journal-Constitution* reported Monday.

"[Mr. Hirsch] was advocating that we explore what is essentially a dead end," Peter Black, the museum's chief historian, told the newspaper.

Museum representatives did not immediately respond to calls by The Associated Press for additional comment Monday.

The four bars of soap, stamped "RIF," were found by a Jewish soldier who was part of a U.S. force that liberated a concentration camp at the end of World War II.

Historians say the initials stand for the German translation of "Reich industrial fat." But at the time the bars were found, the

"I" was widely interpreted as a "J," and the initials were interpreted as standing for *Reines Juden Fett,* or "pure Jewish fat."

The soldier's wife found the soap bars in their basement in 1970, and the couple called a rabbi, who arranged the burial at Atlanta's Greenwood Cemetery. The bars remain buried there.

"There's a religious issue here," Mr. Hirsch said. "These are not just soap. They were buried as if they were human beings."

Mr. Hirsch says his brother was told by their uncle, who has since died, that the Nazis used corpses to make soap.

Mr. Hirsch's memoir, most of which is devoted to his experience as a U.S. soldier in Germany, remains at the museum's bookstore. But the museum distributes a fact sheet saying the contention that Nazis used human corpses for soap is an unsubstantiated rumor.

"This one soap story keeps rolling around," said Deborah Lipstadt, an Emory University history professor who recently prevailed against a libel suit by a British scholar whom she accused of denying the Nazis slaughtered millions of Jews. "Soap became sort of a metaphor—they killed them and made soap out of them—to show how horrible the Nazis were.

"I wouldn't say . . . [the Nazis] never did it. I would leave the door slightly cracked."

The following letter to the editor responds to claims made in the above article.

Dallas Morning News
Oct. 7, 2000
Nazis' Human Soap
Re: "Holocaust museum disputes book's soap account," Sept. 26.

My father was the marshal of the court at the Nuremberg Trials. One of his duties was the safekeeping of exhibits, evidence and witnesses, and seeing that they were at the proper hearings in the courtroom.

On Oct. 4, 1946, three days after the verdicts were read for the "Goering Trial" defendants, my father personally let us, his family, see some of the evidence. I remember my sick feeling in seeing the shrunken head, the lampshade made of human skin displaying a tattoo, and the jar of yellowish human soap made from the concentration camp victims among other proof that was presented in the trials and is documented in their records.

I do not have to rely on my memory alone: it was recorded in my diary I kept while we were in Nuremberg as well as through correspondence and phone conversations with surviving staff who served there. It is also recorded in the trial's official transcript. On transcript Page 16924 of the "Official Transcript of the International Military Tribunal . . . , Chief Justice Lawrence presiding," the first line of the third paragraph records, "After cremation the ashes were used for fertilizer, and in some instances attempts were made to utilize the fat from the bodies of the victims in the commercial manufacture of soap."

The so-called historians who are quoted in the article must have missed this documentation. Surely, they have access to the complete transcript. The judgment presents facts, not allegations, which were proven during the trials. That the Nazis made soap out of human beings is not a "metaphor"; it is a horrible reality. They were seeking to see if they could use the bodies for a source of soap. They removed all gold fillings from the victims' teeth, the clothing off their bodies. They tried horrible medical experiments on human beings we would not submit laboratory mice to. The atrocities by the Nazis were despicable. Assuming this was just a metaphor is blindly ignoring the facts.

Kathy Smith
Dallas

•   •   •

February 11, 1992

Dear Mike,

Thank you so much for the presentation you gave the eating disorder patients on February 5, 1992. I appreciate you reliving your experiences with the patients. It's truly amazing to hear of your courage and having no anger at the ones who did such hideous acts. The story you shared truly touched not only the patients, but me as well.

I think it is truly wonderful how you speak to them, letting them know that they are beautiful. It is really difficult for them to allow themselves to feel good about themselves. Many of the patients have been in their disorder for so long that they've forgotten what a blessing it is to live. You made them think long and hard about the gift they've been given. It's also wonderful for them to hear it from someone not directly associated with the Eating Disorder Program.

Thank you again for working with me on setting up the opportunity to let us come share your history. It was a true pleasure.

Enclosed is a letter from one of our anorexic patients.

> Sincerely,
> Ginger L. Giles
> Therapeutic Recreation Specialist

• • •

[The following letter is the enclosure referred to above by Ms. Giles.]

Dear Mr. Jacobs,

Thanks so much for your presentation and tour of the Holocaust museum. Your positive attitude—after going through such a crisis—brings me a lot of hope. I have had anorexia for 13 years, and it has definitely been a crisis. I have missed out on so much in life. I felt so selfish today, hearing all that you had been through, without choice, but by force. And here, I have had a choice not to starve myself, and I chose to. Food was seen as my enemy, whereas you would have been so happy to have food to eat.

Thanks for your support and your time. You are a very special person!

Sincerely,
L.T.

• • •

Mike recalled the following story regarding another anorexia patient.

One day as I walked through the Valley View Mall in Dallas with my wife and my son Reuben, a teenage girl came running toward us and hugged me. She said to me, "Don't you remember me?"

I said, "Yes, sure." But I really didn't remember her, as I speak to so many people.

She again said, "Don't you remember me?" She finally realized that I didn't remember. She then said, "A week ago you spoke to an eating disorder group of girls that I was in." She said she had listened very carefully to my telling of how I lived during and how I survived the Holocaust as a teenager.

I had asked the group, "When you get up in the morning with no make-up and with curlers in your hair and look into the mirror, who do you see?"

The group was very quiet.

I asked again, "Who do you see?" I then told them, "When you look in the mirror and see yourself, say, 'I'm the most beautiful woman in the world.' Don't let anyone tell you that you are not."

The young woman told me that when she went home, she told her mother that she was not going back to the group. "I am cured," she told her mother.

Her mother said, "What do you mean you are not going back?"

"I am cured," the girl said again.

She told me, "Mother started crying."

As we talked, she called her mother over and said to her, "That's the man who spoke to the group."

The mother grabbed my hand and said, "Thank you for helping my daughter. She is so beautiful and happy—you changed her life."

•   •   •

This letter is from Mike's oldest granddaughter, Rivka. Zaide *is Yiddish for "Grandfather."*

7-8-98

Dear Zaide,

I forget how special you are to me sometimes. I don't know how I could live without you. For the past 15 years, I have taken you for granted. I have never gotten a chance to hear you speak. I totally resent the fact that I haven't sat down, taken notes, and listened to you.

If you were here with me right now at camp, you would be happy that I finally sat down and got through one Holocaust program without having to get up and leave the room. It has taken me a long time to be able to do that. While watching it, all that went through my mind was you. I pictured you and the rest of your family in the slides. It hurts me so much to have to see those slides, because all I can think about is what they did to you. I am slowly letting myself open up and listen to the different stories of the Shoah. I am so sorry that it has taken me this long to be able to listen. In the future, when I am more ready than now to listen, I want to be able to sit and talk with you. I know Leeza, Sarah and Aviva have been able to do it, and I feel so behind.

Please don't get mad at me that I am [un]able to do it, and I have to admit this in a letter. It is just so hard for me to open up my feelings like this. It hurts me so much that I don't have the confidence to listen to you. To me you are the most important thing in the world. I love you so much. I am saying this from the bottom of my heart. I love you.

Love always and forever,
Rivka

• • •

October 11, 2000
Brookhaven College

Dear Mr. Jacob,
I can't tell you how much your talk affected my life. I went back home to my mother's house afterward and told her of the talk. I have been well educated on the Holocaust by my school, but it never really hit me, the horror of it, until I heard you speak yesterday. I think today's society, including myself, has been desensitized to violence. . . I think the Holocaust was almost unreal to me, but hearing you talk made the reality of the inhumanity strike the very core of me. As I spoke with my mother about you, she told me that I had lost relatives in the Holocaust on my father's side. I did not know that my grandfather was Jewish until then. She told me that his mother was Russian and his father was Polish. It has made me very interested in my heritage. I pray that your work will continue to spread and people will continue to hear of the horror of the Holocaust. Not to breed hate, as you said, but to make them aware to never let something like this happen again.

Thank you again.
May the Lord bless you.
Tara Tinsley

• • •

State of Texas
Office of the Governor
September 30, 1994

Greetings to:
Mike Jacobs

As Governor of Texas, it is a great pleasure to congratulate you on earning the Dallas Memorial Center for Holocaust Studies' Hope for Humanity Award and to salute you for years of outstanding service to your community and the citizens of Texas.

It is fitting that you—the driving force behind the Holocaust Center and a champion for Holocaust survivors—are being honored with this award. Like the Phoenix that rose from the ashes, you are living proof that someone with courage, faith and vision can unite and heal people even after unspeakable atrocities have been committed. You have been the guardian of memories—of lost lives, tragic events and horrific scenes—that must not be forgotten, because if we forget, we will wander off the path of renewal and tolerance.

You and the Holocaust Center are indeed beacons of hope for the community, and many look to you for reassurance and support. Your strength is an inspiration to us all, and we salute your tireless efforts to help others break the bonds of prejudice and cruelty. The services you have offered and the selfless acts you perform are invaluable.

On behalf of those whom you have helped, and those who you will help in the future, I offer my deepest gratitude. I am delighted you are being recognized with this award. You've certainly earned it.

> All my best!
> Sincerely,
> Ann W. Richards
> Governor

• • •

Patricia Hesse
Gifted/Talented Coordinator
Weiner Public School
Weiner, AR

November 6, 1998
Dear Ginger and Mike:

It has been almost a year since you were here at our school. I still have students from time to time comment about something that you said. I don't believe there is any way you can possibly know the difference you have made in the world because of your willingness to share of your experience. It is truly a wonderful thing if each of us can touch even one life in a way that lifts that person to a higher and better place—you have done that for countless individuals.

I wanted to tell you about my summer. I went to the Czech Republic and Poland . . . on a trip funded by the Fulbright-Hays Group Projects Abroad. I learned so much about the Holocaust while I was there and did something I never dreamed I would have a chance to do—walk on the hallowed ground [where] so many innocent souls suffered and died. It had a profound effect upon me, both emotionally and spiritually. When we visited Auschwitz, it was a cloudy day with light, misty rain. . . . Our guide was a young teacher (about 33), and she told us many things I had never heard. . . . I had been to the Holocaust Museum in Washington, D.C., but this was much more humbling for me, and I found I could only listen and not speak. When we walked through Hell's Gate at Birkenau, I looked at all the foundations of the now-gone stables and wondered which one you had been in. Everywhere I stepped, I wondered about all those who had stepped there before. I picked up a rock and have it in a place in my home where I can see it every day. It is on a small table, and above it hangs a framed copy of the memorial poem from your museum in Dallas.

Never underestimate the power of your gift. You have not only ensured that countless generations WILL remember, but you have shown the power of love as well—I can think of no higher calling.

Yours sincerely,
Patricia Hesse

• • •

September 25/1986

Dear Mendelek.

At our Waldorf Astoria meeting, you mentioned that you tried to reach Kunow, the place your brother Ruwen was killed together with the other Partisans.

In the Ostrowiec Memorial Book is an article about the 12 Kedoshim murdered by the A.K., and brought to rest in Peace at the Ostrowiec Jewish Cemetery. As the article states: It was a very impressive Funeral.

I, who am the only survivor of mine Family, know that words of Sympathy are meaningless, but I feel that is my duty to enlighten with that article, and clear up you doubts about your brothers burial place.

Wishing you and your family a happy and healthy New Year.

Yours,

Simon Kempinski & Family

• • •

October 29, 1987

Dear Mendelek.

I am late with mailing you the requested photostats.

Mr. Theo Richmond knows, that all of a sudden I got 102+ degrees fever and went to the hospital. It was a minor disorder, and I am almost back to the state of health, before my hospitalization of 13 days. It was a minor thing, but it could not be corrected, before bringing my temperature down to normal.

There are enclosed two (2) sets of photostats and please do not misplace or lose them. You are the only survivor of the Jakubowicz family and you have to carry with pride the torch of your family and especially of Reuben.

I am not trying to preach, but as an old friend, landsman and member of the same Ziouist organization, I am writing those few words from the bottom of my heart. Best Regards for you lovely wife and family.

Yours,

Simon Kempinski

GLOSSARY

A.K.—abbreviation for *Armja Krojowa* ("home army"), pronounced "Armyia Kroyova." The Polish underground group that formed to fight the Germans. This resistance group was directed by the Polish government-in-exile and by its empowered *Delegature* (delegate).

Armja Lodowa—pronounced "Armyia Ludova," meant "People's Army." A resistance group which was supported by the P.P.R., or Polish Workers' Party. The Soviet Union supported this group, as they planned to establish their presence in postwar Poland. The A.K. and the Armyia Ludova were the recognized Polish resistance groups.

Ausweis (German)—identification. Everyone had to carry identification papers.

Augen rechts (German)—command meaning, "Eyes right."

Blockeltester (German)—a prisoner assigned to be in charge of the barracks.

Chalent (Yiddish)—a slowly cooked stew made with beef, potoatoes, beans, and a portion of stuffed cow intestine (like our hotdogs), prepared before sundown and baked on Friday evening until after Sabbath morning services and eaten for Sabbath lunch. The "ch" is pronounced as in English "chair." "Ch" is usually pronounced as a gutteral, hard H in Yiddish.

Challah—special egg bread made for Sabbath with the dough twisted on the top of the loaf.

Chanukah—Jewish festival of lights, takes place in December.

Chazan—cantor.

Cheder—elementary religious school where students learned to read Hebrew, generally geared to prayer, and learned to translate Hebrew to Yiddish, which was generally spoken in the home.

Chevre kadishe—burial society.

Ciotka (Polish)—aunt. Prounounced "tshotsha."

Der Führer (German)—The Leader. Refers to Hitler.

Dummkopf (German)—dumb. Literally, "dumb-head."

Frum—religiously observant.

Geminde (Yiddish)—central committee, in this case of the Jewish community.

Gestapo—German political police during the Nazi era.

Ghetto—a quarter of the city where Jews were required to live.

Goy—Gentile.

Greeven—rendered (cooked in its own fat) chicken or goose fat and pieces of the skin boiled down to browned fat liquid with sliced onions, seasoned with salt.

Groszy—smallest unit of Polish money, like a U.S. penny.

Guten Abend (German)—"Good evening."

Ha-Nerot-Ha-Lalu (Hebrew and Yiddish)—name for a special blessing that is chanted over the **Chanukah** candles as they are lit.

Hasidim—ultra-Orthodox Jews. (Plural of Hasid, sometimes spelled "chasid," pronounced with gutteral, hard "h.")

Hechalutz and **Hapoel** (Hebrew and Yiddish)—names for two Zionist Youth organizations.

Hermann Goeringwerke (German)—"Hermann Goering Works," name of the steel mill in **Ostrowiec**. Hermann Goering was a prominent Nazi politician.

Hora—a Jewish folk dance.

Hutch (Polish)—"Come." Prounounced with hard "h" or "ch" sound.

Jäger—a family name, prononnced "Yager" (long "a").

Jakubowicz—Mike's family name in Polish, pronounced "Yakub-ovitch."

Jude (German)— "Jew," prounced "Yudeh."

Judenrat (German and Yiddish)—a Jewish community council appointed from some of the leadership by the Nazis to take charge of the ghettos. Pronounced "yudenraht."

Kaddish (Hebrew and Yiddish)—Jewish prayer for the dead. Recited at funerals and during periods of mourning. This prayer is also included in morning, evening, Sabbath, and holiday services.

Kanada—a slang term used by prisoners for an area in Birkenau where people coming off the transports into camp had to leave their suitcases with their clothes, food, and valuables. The prisoners called the place Kanada after the country Canada, because it was a good place to work, as they could eat well and had access to the confiscated items, which they had to separate.

Kappo—a prisoner who acted as foreman of a work group.

Kashered (Yiddish and Hebrew)—cleaned and prepared in keeping with Jewish dietary laws.

Kasherut—observance of Jewish dietary laws, keeping **kosher.**

Kiddush—the special blessing that is chanted over wine before Sabbath and a holiday evening meal. Also said in the synagogue before refreshments or lunch after morning services.

Klop (Yiddish)—hit.

Kosher—prepared in keeping with Jewish dietary laws and ritual slaughter of animals.

Kol Nidre—chanted prayer that ushers in **Yom Kippur,** the Day of Atonement, at the evening service.

Khillah—the organized Jewish community.

Kibbutz (Hebrew)—term for a farm cooperative in Israel. It was also a training program for people wanting to immigrate to Israel (then-Palestine) during the British Mandate because of the immigration quota enforced on Jews.

Läusen-Strasse (German)—"Lice Street," or "Lice Promenade."

Luftwaffe (German)—German airforce.

Machorka (Polish)—name of a brand of very strong cigarettes. "Ch" prounced with the hard "h" sound used in "Chanukah."

Matzah—unleavened bread eaten on Passover. Sometimes spelled "matza" or "matzo."

Minyan—the traditional quorum of ten males over the age of thirteen required for a public worship service.

Mojzesz—Polish spelling for the Hebrew and Yiddish name "Moses," also pronounced "Moses."

Ostrowiec—Polish city, prounced "Ostrovitz" in English.

Pesach—Passover.

Rosh Hashana—Jewish New Year holiday.

Ryfka—Mike's sister's name as it was spelled in Poland. English spelling is "Rivka."

SS—German abbreviation for *Schutzstaffel*, or elite guard. The SS was a unit of Nazis created to serve as bodyguards to Hitler. They were later expanded to become regular police, with duties including intelligence work, central security, policing action, and the extermination of undesirables. They were responsible for taking Jews from all over Europe to concentration and death camps.

Salegabetrieb (German)—scrapyard.

Seder—service held during the evening meals during the first two days of **Pesach.**

Shabbas Goy (Yiddish)—a non-Jewish person who would do household chores considered work that Jews could not do on the Sabbath.

Shabbos—Jewish Sabbath, lasting from sundown Friday night until sundown Saturday night.

Sheytl—wig worn by traditionally observant Jewish women after marriage.

Shomer—a watchman, also a man who sits with the body of a deceased person until burial.

Shochet—the man who slaughters an animal to be eaten, according to Jewish ritual, which must be painless to the animal.

Shtibel—a small house of prayer, usually chasidic (ultra-Orthodox), and also very observant.

Shul—synagogue.

Simcha—joyous celebration.

Simchat Torah—Hebrew and Yiddish (Simchas) name for the holiday rejoicing over the completion of the reading and beginning the new cycle of reading the Torah (Five Books of Moses) through the year.

Sonderkommando (German)—Male prisoners who removed bodies from gas chambers and took them to crematoria or pits to be burned.

Spiritus—100 percent alcohol made from potatoes.

Stehen bleiben (German)—command meaning, "Remain standing."

Stoje (Polish)—"Stop." Pronounced "stoye."

Szlama—Polish spelling for the Hebrew and Yiddish name "Schlomo."

Talis—(pronounced "Talit" in Israel) prayer shawl.

Tefillin (Hebrew and Yiddish)—phylacteries, two small black leather boxes with black leather straps attached to them. The boxes contain excerpts from the Five Books of Moses that stress the duty of Jews to love and serve God with "all their heart" and to remember and practice loving kindness. One box is strapped to the left arm, close to the heart, and the other box is strapped on the forehead, close to the brain or mind. Tefillin are to be worn during weekday morning services by all males over the age of thirteen, serving as a reminder of proper behavior.

Tepper Marik (Yiddish)—market square. Literally, "pot market."

Trager (Yiddish)—a porter (pronounced with a long "a").

Treyf—non-**kosher** food, not acceptable in Jewish tradition.

Volksdeutscher—an "ethnic German" loyal to Hitler and the Nazi party.

Warta (Polish)—river name, pronounced "Varta."

Yarmulke (Yiddish)—skull cap worn at all times by very orthodox Jewish men, generally work by men in the synagogue nd by some in reform temples.

Yeshiva—Rabbinic seminary.

Yizkor—Remembrance, the name for the special memorial service that is included during four of the holiday services.

Yom Kippur—Day of Atonement.

Yom Tov (Yiddish and Hebrew)—Jewish holiday.

Yortzayt—anniversary of a death, when **kaddish** is said for immediate family members.

Zigeuner (German and Yiddish)—Gypsy. Prounounced "tsugoiner" in German, "tsugeiner" in Yiddish.

Zloty—Polish unit of money similar to U.S. dollar, made up of 100 **groszy.**

Notes and Further Reading

Books:
Mike is quoted in the following books:

Berenbaum, Michael. *The World Must Know: The History of the Holocaust as Told in the United States Holocaust Memorial Museum.* New York: Little, Brown, & Company. Pp. 147, 149.

Richmond, Theo. *Konin: One Man's Quest for a Vanished Jewish Community.* New York: Pantheon, 1995. Pp. 167, 175, 193, 321, 306–307, 318–319, 308–309. (Originally published in hardback as *Konin: A Quest.* Chapter 46 is about Mike.)

Winegarten, Ruthe, and Cathy Schecter. *Deep in the Heart: The Lives and Legends of Texas Jews.* Eakin Press, 1990. P. 161.

Oral History Collections:
Mike is included in the following oral history collections:

Fortunoff Video Archive for Holocaust Testimonies, Yale Universtiy, 1997.

Holocaust Survivor Video Testimony Tape Collection of Dallas Memorial Center for Holocaust Studies.

Oral History Collection of University of North Texas, no. 831, Interview with Mike Jacobs, November 26, 1989.

Survivors of the SHOAH (Holocaust) Visual History Foundation, Interview with Mike (or Michael) Jacobs, founded and funded by Stephen Spielberg.

Video Archive for Holocaust Testomonies at Yale Sterling Memorial Library, 1985.

Newspapers:
Dallas Morning News—High Profile, by Lori Stahl. Sunday, February 17, 1991.
See a selection of news articles in Appendix 3, which begins on page 195.

Participation in Holocaust Remembrance on a National Level:

Mike participated in and has been recognised for his contribution by the United States Holocaust Museum Campaign to Remember.

Mike serves on the National Board of the American Gathering of Jewish Holocaust Surviviors.

Mike and Ginger participated in the Unites States Holocaust Museum's Journey to Western Europe in November of 1992, which was also sponsored by the U.S. Defense Department. The journey included memorial ceremonies at Beendonck, Belgium, Drancy, Holocaust memorials in Paris, and Omaha Beach, Normandy, France, along with collecting and bringing soil back from Buchenwald and Mauthausen concentration camps (the soil was for the museum).

Extension of a Dream:

As of September 2000, more than 60,000 people visit the Dallas Memorial Center for Holocaust Studies annually.

Many teachers specifically ask for Mike Jacobs to take their classes and groups through the Center.

The Dallas Memorial Center for Holocaust Studies is now Dallas Holocaust Museum-Center for Education and Tolerance. It is now more centrally located in the west end of downtown Dallas temporarily at 211 N. Record St., Suite 100, Dallas, Texas 75202-3361, Phone 214-741-7500. The website is www.dallasholocaustmuseum.org

A large state-of-the-art building is being planned nearby.

Further Reading:

Books that address some of the incidents that Mike experienced, that he was told of by some of the sonderkommandos he was in camp with, has spoken of since 1956, and that he writes about, include the following:

Czech, Danuta. *Auschwitz Chronicle, 1939–1945*. From the Archives of The Auschwitz Memorial and The German Federal Archives. New York: Henry Holt and Company, Inc., First Owl Book Edition, 1997.

Dawidowicz, Lucy S. *The War Against The Jews, 1933–1945*. New York: Holt, Rinehart, and Winston, 1975.

Gilbert, Martin. *The Holocaust; A History of the Jews of Europe During the Second World War*. New York: Holt, Rinehart, and Winston, 1986.

———. *Final Journey: The Fate of the Jews in Nazi Europe*. London: George Rainbird Ltd., 1979.

———. *The Macmillan Atlas of the Holocaust*. New York: Macmillan, 1982.

Hilberg, Raul. *The Destruction of the European Jews*. Chicago: Quadrangle Books, 1967.

Lawliss, Charles. . . . *and God Cried: The Holocaust Remembered*. New York: JG Press, 1994.